In the
FOOTSTEPS
of the SAVIOR

FOLLOWING JESUS THROUGH
THE HOLY LAND

BIBLE STUDY GUIDE | SIX SESSIONS

MAX LUCADO

with ANDREA RAMSAY

HarperChristian
Resources

In the Footsteps of the Savior Bible Study Guide
© 2023 by Max Lucado

Requests for information should be addressed to:
HarperChristian Resources, 3900 Sparks Dr. SE, Grand Rapids, Michigan 49546

ISBN 978-0-310-16383-1 (softcover)
ISBN 978-0-310-16384-8 (ebook)

First Printing February 2023 / Printed in the United States of America

23 24 25 26 27 LBC 6 5 4 3 2

Contents

A NOTE FROM MAX LUCADO

There's something significant about knowing the location where an important event took place. Just think about when a friend is telling you a riveting story. What do you want to know? You want to know *where* it happened. You want to know what the *surroundings* were like. You want to be able to *picture yourself there* so you can better understand what actually happened.

It's the same with the stories you read in the Bible. When you know where Jesus' miracles, sermons, and interactions actually took place, you can put yourself there. You can see what Jesus saw. You can feel what he felt. You can hear what he heard. You can better understand what was happening in the world of his day . . . which can help you better understand why Jesus did what he did and said what he said. The location adds context.

Recently, I had the opportunity to visit places in Israel where many of the stories we read about in the Gospels and Acts took place. Locations such as Capernaum, the Sea of Galilee, the Mount of Beatitudes, the Temple Steps and Garden Tomb in Jerusalem, and the coastal town of Caesarea Maritima. As you go through this study, you will see what these places look like today and hear a story from the Bible about what happened there. It is my hope that seeing these them will help you better experience the people and places that shaped Jesus' life.

What's more, it is my goal that seeing these places will help you to connect with Jesus' *humanity*. The Bible states that Jesus was born in a *real* town called Bethlehem, walked on *real* roads in Israel, travelled by boat on a *real* lake in Galilee, taught the people from a *real* hillside known as the Mount of Beatitudes, spoke to many others from the steps of a *real* temple in Jerusalem, and finally was crucified and rose again from a *real* tomb in that same city. None of these places were invented . . . for as you will see in this study, you can visit them today.

God has more in store for you than you can imagine. I'm praying this study will give you a life-altering encounter with him as we walk *In the Footsteps of the Savior*.

—MAX LUCADO

How to Use This Guide

Grab your passport and pack your bags. You are about to embark on an adventure through some of the most prominent cities, towns, and locations in the New Testament. Why are these places so important? It's because Jesus and the disciples were there.

This study will take you to some of the important places where key events in the Gospels and Acts took place. You will visit the city of Capernaum, where Jesus raised a girl to life. The Sea of Galilee, where Jesus walked on water. The Mount of Beatitudes, where Jesus told the people to trust God and not worry. The Temple Steps in Jerusalem, near the place where Jesus had a conversation with a Pharisee at night. The Garden Tomb, believed by many to be where Jesus rose from the dead. And the city of Caesarea by the Sea, where the disciple Peter received an important lesson on who is "in" and "out" of God's kingdom.

Before you begin this journey, keep in mind there are few ways you can work through this material. You can experience this study with others in a group (such as a Bible study, Sunday school class, or any other small-group gathering), or you may choose to study the content on your own. Either way, the videos for each session are available for you to view at any time by following the instructions provided on the inside cover of this study guide.

Group Study

Each session is divided into two parts: (1) a group study section, and (2) a personal study section. The group study section provides a basic framework on how to open your time together, get the most out of the video content, and discuss the key ideas together that were presented in the teaching. Each session includes the following:

- **Welcome:** A short note about the topic of the session for you to read on your own before you meet together as a group.
- **Connect:** A few icebreaker questions to get you and your group members thinking about the topic and interacting with each other.

- **Watch:** An outline of the key points that will be covered in each video teaching to help you follow along, stay engaged, and take notes.
- **Discuss:** Questions to help your group reflect on the material presented and apply it to your lives. In each session, you will be given four suggested questions and four additional questions to use as time allows.
- **Respond:** A short personal exercise to help reinforce the key ideas.
- **Pray:** A place for you to record prayer requests and praises for the week.

If you are doing this study in a group, have your own copy of this study guide so you can write down your thoughts, responses, and reflections and have access to the videos via streaming. You will also want to have a copy of the *In the Footsteps of the Savior* book, as reading it alongside the curriculum will provide you with deeper insights. (See the notes at the beginning of each group session and personal study section on which chapters of the book you should read before the next group session.) Finally, keep these points in mind:

- **Facilitation:** If you are doing this study in a group, you will want to appoint someone to serve as a facilitator. This person will be responsible for starting the video and keeping track of time during discussions and activities. If *you* have been chosen for this role, there are some resources in the back of this guide that can help you lead your group through the study.

- **Faithfulness:** Your small group is a place where tremendous growth can happen as you reflect on the Bible, ask questions, and learn what God is doing in other people's lives. For this reason, be fully committed and attend each session so you can build trust and rapport with the other members.

- **Friendship:** The goal of any small group is to serve as a place where people can share, learn about God, and build friendships. So seek to make your group a "safe place." Be honest about your thoughts and feelings . . . but also listen carefully to everyone else's thoughts, feelings, and opinions. Keep anything personal that your group members share in confidence so that you can create a community where people can heal, be challenged, and grow spiritually.

If you are studying on your own, read the opening Welcome section and reflect on the questions in the Connect section. Watch the video and use the prompts provided to take notes. Finally, personalize the questions and exercises in the Discuss and Respond sections. Close by recording any requests you want to pray about during the week.

PERSONAL STUDY

As the name implies, the personal study is for you to experience on your own during the week. Each exercise is designed to help you explore the key ideas you uncovered during your group time and delve into passages of Scripture that will help you apply those principles to your life. Go at your own pace, doing a little each day or all at once, and spend a few moments in silence to listen to what God might be saying to you. Each personal study includes:

- **Open:** A brief introduction to lead you into the personal study for the day.
- **Read:** A few passages on the topic of the day for you to read and review.
- **Reflect:** Questions for you to answer related to the passages you just read.
- **Pray:** A prompt to help you express what you've studied in a prayer to God.

If you are doing this study as part of a group, and you are unable to finish (or even start) these personal studies for the week, you should still attend the group time. Be assured that you are still wanted and welcome even if you don't have your "homework" done. The group studies and personal studies are intended to help you hear what God wants you to hear and how to apply what he is saying to your life. Be listening for him to speak to you as you learn about what it means to trust in Jesus in every area of your life.

WEEK 1

BEFORE GROUP MEETING	Read chapters 6–7 of *In the Footsteps of the Savior* Read the Welcome section (page 3)
GROUP MEETING	Discuss the Connect questions Watch the video teaching for session 1 Discuss the questions that follow as a group Do the closing exercise and pray (pages 4–12)
PERSONAL STUDY – DAY 1	Complete the daily study (pages 14–15)
PERSONAL STUDY – DAY 2	Complete the daily study (pages 16–17)
PERSONAL STUDY – DAY 3	Complete the daily study (pages 18–19)
PERSONAL STUDY – DAY 4	Complete the daily study (pages 20–22)
PERSONAL STUDY – DAY 5 (before week 2 group meeting)	Complete the daily study (page 23) Read chapter 5 of *In the Footsteps of the Savior* Complete any unfinished personal studies

CAPERNAUM

FOLLOWING JESUS WHEN YOU DOUBT

*While Jesus was still speaking, some people came from the house
of Jairus, the synagogue leader. "Your daughter is dead," they said.
"Why bother the teacher anymore?" Overhearing what they said,
Jesus told him, "Don't be afraid; just believe."*

MARK 5:35-36

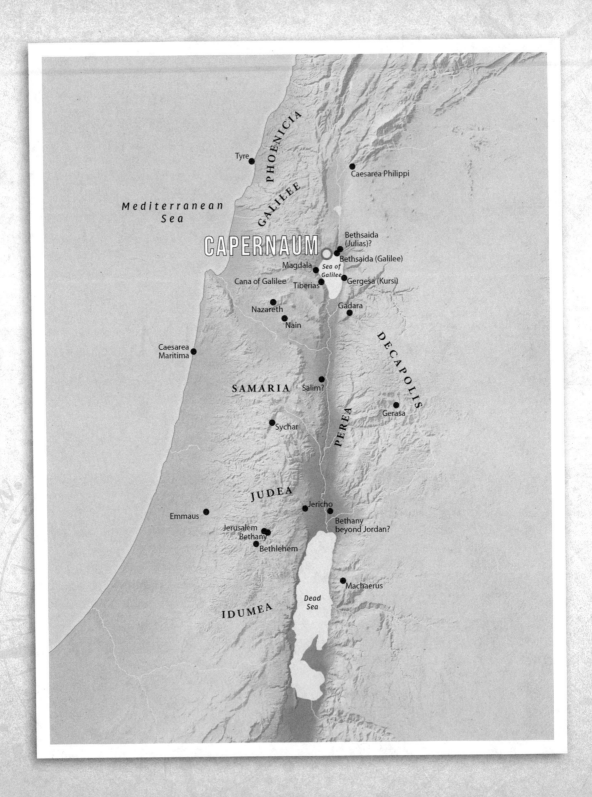

Welcome | READ ON YOUR OWN

How often have you wondered if Jesus *can*? Is he capable of doing what you ask? How powerful is he? You need a miracle, but you've never witnessed one.

Perhaps you know he can, but you wonder if he will. He told you he would. At one time in your life, you trusted him deeply. But things have changed. Will Jesus still show up for you today?

And how often have you wondered if Jesus cares? Why ask when you don't even know if he will listen? And why should he? You're you. Nothing special. So many others in the world need more than you do.

No matter where you come from, whether you are known and respected in your community or marginalized and alone, Jesus' miracles in Capernaum that you'll learn about in this session can teach you this: He cares about you. He can bring you the healing you need. And he will come to you.

No one is too lowly for him to heal, and no one is too well off.

The stories you'll study in this session confirm this. They tell us that he will, even if the timing is different from what we were expecting. And they tell us that Jesus cares. You don't have to earn his attention or affection. As his child, it is already yours.

Connect | 15 MINUTES

If you or any of your group members don't know each other, take a few minutes to introduce yourselves. Then, to get things started, discuss one of the following questions:

- Why did you decide to join this study? What do you hope to learn?

— *or* —

- Have you ever witnessed or experienced a miracle? If so, what was it?

Watch | 20 MINUTES

Now it's time to watch the video for this session, which you can access by playing the DVD or through streaming (see the instructions provided on the inside front cover). As you watch, use the following outline to record any thoughts or concepts that stand out to you.

I. Jairus pleads with Jesus to heal his daughter

    A. *Do you think he can? Do you think he cares? Do you think he'll come?* Jairus shrugs his shoulders in desperation. He says, "I do not know what he will do, but I do not know what else to do."

    B. When Jairus sees Christ, he falls to his knees and begs, "'My dear daughter is at death's door. Come and lay hands on her so she will get well and live" (Mark 5:23 MSG).

    C. Jesus' instant willingness moistens the eyes of Jairus. A sun ray of hope falls upon his shadowed heart. He dares to think, *Jesus can help. Jesus does care. Jesus will come.*

II. Jesus stops when the bleeding woman touches his cloak

    A. In the woman's mind is the thought: *If I can just touch the hem of him.* For twelve years, she has been untouchable, going from doctor to doctor. She's dead broke and has no hope.

    B. The divinity of Christ is ahead of the humanity of Christ. He feels a rush go out, and she feels a rush go in. Jesus says, "Something just happened." Such a fascinating moment.

    C. The woman said not a word aloud, and yet the healing came. She inches her way toward Christ. "Jesus waited as "she told him the whole story" (Mark 5:33 CEV).

    D. Jairus doesn't know whether to interrupt what's happening or to give up on Christ. But then a servant arrives and says, "Your daughter is dead. Why trouble the Teacher any further?" (Mark 5:35 NKJV).

III. Jesus tells Jairus to not be afraid but just believe

    A. Jairus has an answer to his questions—*I wonder if he can; I wonder if he cares; I wonder if he'll come.* And he doesn't like the answers.

    B. Jesus cleared out the mourners. He wanted the presence of faith. Then he turned his attention to the body of the girl. And the questions surface again. *Does he care?*

    C. Jesus was listening to the story of the woman who had been healed. He was surrounded by his disciples. He was surrounded by all the people. But he had not forgotten Jairus.

    D. "He took the child by the hand, and said to her, '*Talitha, cumi*,' which is translated, 'Little girl, I say to you, arise.' Immediately the girl arose and walked" (Mark 5:41–42 NKJV).

CAPERNAUM

CAPERNAUM

The town of Capernaum was likely established during the second century BC, when a number of other small fishing villages began to spring up around the Sea of Galilee. The original name of the town was *Kfar Nahum,* which means "village of comfort" in Hebrew. In Jesus' day, it was one of the main trading centers in the region, with travelers, caravans, and traders passing through it as they journeyed along the Via Maris, the main Roman road in the region.

Archaeological excavations in Capernaum, dating back to 1838, have revealed the ruins of a synagogue and first-century houses. The synagogue was likely constructed in the fourth to fifth century AD, but beneath its foundation lies another one made of basalt, which many believe to be the original foundation of the synagogue mentioned in the Gospels.

The group of houses, located between the synagogue and the Sea of Galilee, appear to have been occupied until the fourth century AD. One of the houses appears to have been modified during the latter half of the first century to serve as a large communal gathering place. Some have concluded that this reveals the home was venerated from early times as the home of Simon Peter and that the early Christians met there for some time.[1]

SIGNIFICANT EVENTS THAT TOOK PLACE IN CAPERNAUM	
Jesus amazes the crowds with his teaching	Mark 1:21–22
Jesus commands an evil spirit to leave a man	Mark 1:23–26
Jesus calls Peter, Andrew, James, and John to follow him	Matthew 4:18–22
Jesus calls Matthew to follow him	Matthew 9:9–13
The faith of a Roman centurion amazes Jesus	Luke 7:1–10
A woman with an issue of blood is healed	Luke 8:43–48
Jesus brings the daughter of the synagogue leader to life	Luke 8:49–56
Jesus heals a paralytic man and forgives his sins	Matthew 9:1–8
Jesus heals Peter's mother-in-law	Mark 1:29–31
Jesus gives a sermon in the synagogue on the bread of life	John 6:25–59
Jesus rebukes Capernaum for the people's unrepentant hearts	Matthew 11:20–24

IV. What Jesus is saying to us through this story

    A. Jesus wanted to do more than just raise the dead. He wanted to show us that he cares and that he can. But he also wanted us to know that he comes. He comes in the form of encouragement. He comes in the form of help. He comes in the form of kindness.

    B. What is Jesus saying to us through this story? *Don't be afraid. Just believe.*

    C. We all wonder if the affection of God will get turned off. But to those concerns, the Scripture says, "For as the heavens are high above the earth, so great is His mercy toward those who fear Him; as far as the east is from the west, so far has He removed our transgressions from us. As a father pities his children, so the the LORD pities those who fear Him" (Psalm 103:11–13 NKJV).

Discuss | 35 MINUTES

Take some time to discuss what you just watched by answering the following questions. There are some suggested questions below to help you begin your discussion, but feel free to pick any of the additional questions as well as time allows.

Suggested Questions

1. Ask someone in the group to read the story of Jairus and his daughter and the bleeding woman in Mark 5:21–43. How did Jairus and the bleeding woman approach Jesus differently? Why do you think they approached him the way they did?

2. Why do you think Jesus spent so much time with the bleeding woman, listening to her story when she had broken several social laws to touch him? What does this tell you about how Jesus feels about those who exist in "the margins"?

3. The Bible reveals that the woman who reached out and touched Jesus' cloak then told Christ "her whole story" (Mark 5:33 CEV). What do you think she included in her story? How would it feel for you to sit with Jesus and tell him your whole story?

4. Jairus had to wait for Jesus to heal his daughter. Have you ever had to wait on Jesus' healing? What meaning or purpose have you found in that time of waiting?

Additional Questions

5. Take a moment to review Mark 5:35–42 again. Why did the people in Jairus' household laugh at Jesus? How do you think you would have reacted in this situation?

6. What did Jesus do with the people who laughed? Why do you think he did this? When it comes to faith and belief, how are you affected by those around you?

7. Where do you need healing in your life today? (This could be physical healing, emotional, or relational—whatever feels sick or broken.)

8. What do you have trouble believing the most: that Jesus *cares*, that he will *come*, or that he *can*? Explain your response.

Respond | 10 MINUTES

Review the outline for the video teaching and any notes you took. In the space below, write down your most significant takeaway from this session.

Pray | 10 MINUTES

Praying for one another is one of the most important things you can do as a community. So use this time wisely and make it more than just a "closing prayer" to end your group experience. Be intentional about sharing your prayers, reviewing how God is answering your prayers, and actually praying for each other as a group. Use the space below to write down any requests so that you and your group members can continue to pray about them in the week ahead.

Name   Request

Personal Study

You are on a journey toward a better understanding of the lives that Jesus touched while he lived on this earth . . . and what that means for you. A key part of this understanding involves studying Scripture. This is the goal of these personal studies—to help you explore what the Bible has to say and how to apply God's Word to your life. As you work through each of these exercises, be sure to write down your responses to the questions, as you will be given a few minutes to share your insights at the start of the next session if you are doing this study with others. If you are reading *In the Footsteps of the Savior* alongside this study, first read chapters 6–7. (You can also read chapters 1–3 for some background information on Jesus' early years.)

APPROACHING THE LORD

Jairus and the woman approached Jesus differently. Jairus approached him directly: "When he saw Jesus, he fell at his feet. He pleaded earnestly with him, 'My little daughter is dying. Please come and put your hands on her so that she will be healed and live'" (Mark 5:22–23). The woman approached him indirectly: "She came up behind him in the crowd and touched his cloak, because she thought, 'If I just touch his clothes, I will be healed'" (Mark 5:27–28).

Neither way was wrong or right. Most likely, the way they approached Christ had to do with their stations in life. Jairus was a respected leader in the community. The bleeding woman was an outcast from society based on Jewish law. She shouldn't have been out on the street in public, much less touching the tassels of Jesus' cloak. She probably feared that if she approached Jesus directly, she would be denied, as it was against the law for him to touch her.

Sometimes we approach Jesus boldly. We know what we need and believe that he can give it to us. Other times, we approach Jesus hesitantly. We're afraid to ask for what we need because we don't think we deserve it or we're unsure he will give it to us. We can learn something from Jairus and the bleeding woman. It doesn't matter what state we're in when we approach Christ—desperate, doubting, bold, or uncertain. What matters is that we *approach* him. We come to him as we are and ask him for what we need. He will not turn us away.

READ | Hebrews 4:14–16

REFLECT

1. When Jesus died on the cross, the veil in the temple tore in two (see Matthew 27:51). This veil separated two rooms in the temple: the Holy of Holies and the Holy Place. The Holy of Holies held the Ark of the Covenant, where God dwelled. Only the high priest could enter the Holy of Holies, and only once a year on the

Day of Atonement when he made sacrifices to atone for the people's sin. Knowing this, what does it mean for Jesus to be our high priest? According to this passage, what kind of high priest is he?

2. Because Jesus is our high priest, how does the author of Hebrews say that we can approach God's throne? What will we find there?

3. Take an inventory of yourself. How are you feeling? What thoughts are going through your mind? What has happened today that has impacted you? Considering this, how would you approach God's throne right now—just as you are?

4. What do you need to bring before the Lord today? Do you feel confident bringing this before him, or uncertain, or worried, or something else? Explain your response.

PRAY | End your time in prayer. Come before the Lord just as you are. Tell him what you need. Be assured that your great high priest has paved the way for you to come before God's throne with confidence so that you can receive his grace and mercy.

-Day 2-

BROUGHT INTO BELONGING

According to Jewish law, the bleeding woman was unclean (see Leviticus 15:25–28). This meant she had to remain isolated from her community and no one could touch her until she was determined to be clean again. You can imagine that if she had been isolated for twelve years, she hadn't talked to many people. Who had listened to her in that time? Where did she belong? What community took her in despite her being unclean? It's reasonable to believe no one.

Historians speculate that her sickness started soon after puberty, which means she had lived most of her adult life in isolation, growing up through adolescence and young adulthood alone.[2] Until Jesus. Jesus saw her and listened to her. The Bible says that she "came trembling with fear and knelt down in front of Jesus . . . then she told him the whole story" (Mark 5:33 CEV).

Her *whole* story. How transforming it must have been to be heard—and not just for a minute but for as long as it took to tell her entire story. Then Jesus took things a step further. He said to her, "Daughter, your faith has healed you. Go in peace and be freed from your suffering" (verse 34). By calling her daughter, he was reincorporating her into the community.[3] Jesus healed the woman physically but also emotionally. By listening to her and bringing her back into societal acceptance, he brought her out of isolation and into belonging.

READ | Isaiah 43:1–7

REFLECT

1. In this passage, the prophet Isaiah is conveying a prophetic promise from God to his people. Even though they would be scattered by the Babylonian captivity, he

would bring them back from exile and redeem them. How does God relate to the Israelites in this passage? What does he call them? How does he describe them?

2. The Lord promises that he will be with his people when they "pass through the waters" and "walk through the fire" (verse 2). What do you think the "waters" and "the fire" represent? What is God saying to his people by making this promise?

3. God tells his people that they are "precious and honored in his sight" (verse 4). What does God say he is willing to do to redeem them from their captors?

4. This promise for the Israelites is also a prophecy for us. Christ will redeem us and call us by name. How does it feel to know that God considers you a part of his own family—that you are his son or daughter? How could this give you a sense of belonging?

PRAY | Read these words again in Isaiah 43:1–7 and pray through it for your prayer time. Personalize it as if God is speaking directly to you . . . because he is.

Day 3

TRUSTING CHRIST IN THE PAUSE

We talked in this session about "the pause" . . . that moment right after you hear the bad news. Your loved one is sick. You didn't get the part. You're being laid off. These are heavy moments in which you are trying to process some devastating news. A moment that Jairus experienced when a servant told him, "Your daughter is dead. . . . Why bother the teacher anymore?" (Mark 5:35).

This tends to be our reaction in the pause—to give up and stop trying. But it's in the pause that Jesus springs to action: "Overhearing what they said, Jesus told him, 'Don't be afraid; just believe'" (verse 36). What did Jairus think of this? Perhaps he hardly heard Jesus, as he was running back home to see if the news was true. Perhaps he was frozen in disbelief and Jesus' words simply reverberated in his head. Or maybe . . . he felt comforted. Maybe these words uttered by the divine gave him a glimmer of hope. Perhaps he trusted Christ.

We don't know how Jairus felt about Jesus' words. But we know what he *didn't* do. He didn't deny Jesus entry into his home or prevent Jesus from seeing his daughter. He allowed Jesus to return with him, and because of this, Jesus was able to prove that he *cared* about his daughter, that he *could* heal his daughter, and that he *would* heal her. This doesn't always happen in our stories. Our pauses do not always turn into rejoicing. But that doesn't mean that Jesus isn't still with us, comforting us and whispering, "Don't be afraid; just believe."

READ | 2 Corinthians 1:3–7

REFLECT

1. The apostle Paul had seen his share of suffering. In other places in this letter, he talks about being persecuted for his faith and dealing with a "thorn" in his side—some type of physical, spiritual, or emotional affliction (or something else entirely) that kept tormenting him (see 12:7). His message to the church on comfort and suffering was

counter to the philosophy of the day that taught people should ignore their pain.[4] What connection does Paul make between comfort and suffering in this passage?

2, Paul encourages the believers with his reassurance that God "comforts us in all our troubles" (verse 4). However, this is not just for our own benefit. What does Paul say we should do when we are comforted? How does this strengthen the body of Christ?

3, Paul says that his sufferings and distress serve a purpose. "If we are distressed, it is for your comfort and salvation; if we are comforted, it is for your comfort, which produces in you patient endurance of the same sufferings we suffer" (verse 6). What do you think enabled Paul to view his trials and struggles in this way?

4, Think about the trials you are facing. Where do you need Jesus' comfort today? How could his words—"don't be afraid; just believe"—apply in that situation?

PRAY | Ask God for comfort, however you need it. Ask him to help you believe. Ask him to help you not be afraid. Feel comforted by Christ's words today.

DEALING WITH DOUBTERS

When Jesus arrived at Jairus' home, friends and family had gathered to mourn the death of Jairus' daughter. Jesus asked, "Why all this commotion and wailing? The child is not dead but asleep" (Mark 5:39). The mourners responded by laughing at him. Jesus responded by putting them out. The Greek word used here is *ekballo*, which means to cast out or drive out.[5]

Jesus didn't need their scoffing as he performed his miracle . . . and neither do we. We don't need to surround ourselves with people who scoff at our faith, at us, or at our hopes. You've probably been in groups like this before. It can affect your faith in God and in yourself. But the opposite is also true. When you're surrounded by people who have faith in God and have faith in you, you then have faith in yourself. You feel uplifted and encouraged.

Jesus surrounded himself with all kinds of people—fishermen, the poor, the sick, the doubters. But he didn't surround himself with those who laughed at him, doubted him, or had no faith in him. In the same way, who we spend our time with *matters*.

This doesn't mean we must always be surrounded by perfect people (which isn't possible) or we must always be surrounded by other Christians (which would be counter to Christ's teaching and actions). But it does mean we pay attention to our environment. Is it supportive? Is it encouraging? Does the group encourage you to grow in your faith? If the answer to these questions is *no*, then it's time to surround ourselves with people who will.

READ | Galatians 5:13–26

REFLECT

1. The church in Galatia was struggling with the tension of being Jews who followed the law and now being Christians who followed Jesus. A group of teachers (known as the "Judaizers") were preaching that followers of Christ still needed to be circumcised and

also follow the Hebrew law. Paul's goal in this letter was to put this argument to rest, remind the church of how they were to treat each other, and emphasize they no longer had to follow the law to receive grace. Instead, the grace they already received from Christ would produce the fruit needed to build a loving and secure community. How does Paul sum up the most important "law" for believers to keep (see verses 13–15)?

2. Paul makes a sharp contrast between the "acts of the flesh" and the "fruit of the Spirit" (see verses 19–23). What are some of the traits of the acts of the flesh? What are some of the traits of the fruits of the Spirit? How are these fruits developed?

3. When you look at your circle of friends and relationships, what kind of people are you surrounded by? How do you treat each other? How do these people affect you?

4. What fruit do you see in your church or community, if any? Would you like your community to produce more fruit? If so, what kind?

PRAY | Be honest with God about how the people you are surrounding yourself with are impacting your life. Thank him for a strong community that encourages you, or ask him to bring you an encouraging and supportive community to help you grow closer to Christ.

CATCH UP AND REFLECT

Use this time to go back and complete any study and reflection questions from previous days this week that you weren't able to finish. Make a note below of any revelations you've had and reflect on any growth or personal insights you've gained.

Spend the next two days reading chapter 5 of *In the Footsteps of the Savior*. Use the space below to record anything in the chapters that stands out to you or encourages you.

WEEK 2

BEFORE GROUP MEETING	Read chapter 5 of *In the Footsteps of the Savior* Read the Welcome section (page 27)
GROUP MEETING	Discuss the Connect questions Watch the video teaching for session 2 Discuss the questions that follow as a group Do the closing exercise and pray (pages 28–34)
PERSONAL STUDY - DAY 1	Complete the daily study (pages 36–37)
PERSONAL STUDY - DAY 2	Complete the daily study (pages 38–39)
PERSONAL STUDY - DAY 3	Complete the daily study (pages 40–41)
PERSONAL STUDY - DAY 4	Complete the daily study (pages 42–44)
PERSONAL STUDY - DAY 5 (before week 3 group meeting)	Complete the daily study (page 45) Read chapter 4 of *In the Footsteps of the Savior* Complete any unfinished personal studies

SEA OF GALILEE

FOLLOWING JESUS IN YOUR STORMS

*A furious squall came up, and the waves broke over the boat,
so that it was nearly swamped. Jesus was in the stern,
sleeping on a cushion. The disciples woke him and said to him,
"Teacher, don't you care if we drown?"*

MARK 4:37-38

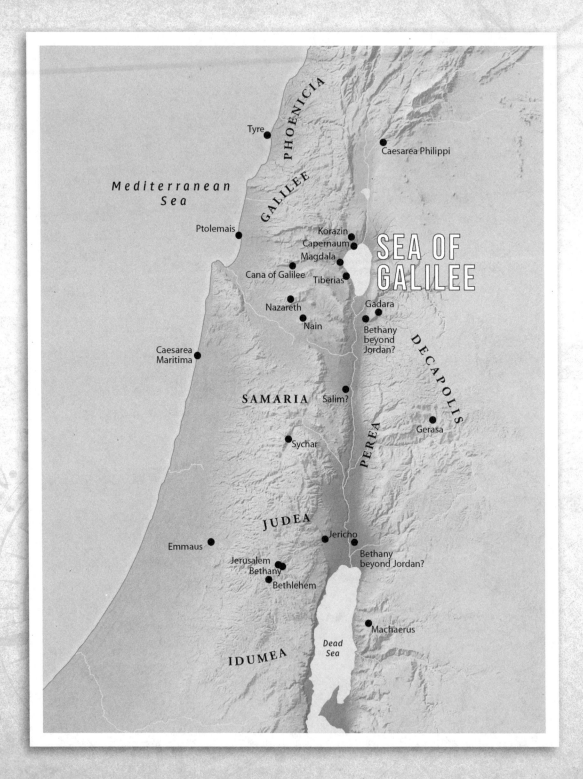

Welcome | READ ON YOUR OWN

Where does life find you today? Under clear skies? Creeping into darker waters? Or smack dab in the middle of a storm? Perhaps it feels as if the storm has been raging for days, weeks, years. You can't remember the last time you experienced calm waters or saw blue skies.

Or maybe you just got through one storm only to find another one looming on the horizon. Back-to-back squalls. Nature can be so cruel. *Life* can be so cruel.

Jesus said to his followers, "In this world you will have trouble" (John 16:33). In other words, *life comes with storms*. The atmospheric conditions of this fallen world create a low-pressure system that generates struggles, stress, challenges. Trials sweep into our lives and transform what was once calm and tranquil into turbulent and chaotic. As the winds continue to rage, we wonder if God is aware of our storm . . . and if he will see us through it.

The disciples in this week's story found themselves in a literal storm as they followed Jesus' instructions to get into a boat and travel to the opposite side of the Sea of Galilee. They had reason to be afraid. They had reason to fear for their lives. And as the winds continued to rage, they had reason to wonder if Jesus knew of their plight and would see them through it.

In this session, you will dig deeper into the disciples' experience. You will explore how it parallels the storms you are facing. And you will discover that Jesus is present when the storms are at their peak—and that he calls you to take courage in the great I Am.

Connect | 15 MINUTES

Take a few minutes to get better acquainted with your fellow group members. Then choose one of the following questions to discuss as a group:

- What is a key insight or takeaway from last week's personal study that you would like to share with the group?

— *or* —

- How do you tend to respond when you see trouble looming on the horizon?

Watch | 20 MINUTES

Now watch the video for this session (remember that you can access this video via streaming by following the instructions printed on the inside front cover). As you watch, use the following outline to record any thoughts or concepts that stand out to you.

I. The nature of storms on the Sea of Galilee

    A. The diminutive state of the Sea of Galilee makes it more subjective to the winds that howl down on the water out of the Golan Heights. It turns this relatively calm body of water into a blender of ten-foot waves. It can happen several times over the course of a winter.

    B. This is the situation in which the disciples found themselves. The lake became a popcorn popper, lifting their boat, spinning it around, plopping it down.

    C. The fishermen among the disciples knew what was about to happen. So they start rowing. They row, row, row the boat. But they do not get far, because they're rowing into the wind.

II. The nature of storms in our lives

   A. Life comes with storms. No one gets through scot-free. Not the old, not the young, not the rich, not the poor, not the healthy, not the unhealthy. Everybody has to face storms.

   B. Peter and his fellow storm-riders knew they were in trouble. They knew what these storms could do. They had weathered them before.

   C. "Has anyone seen Jesus? He *told* us to get into the boat." It's one thing to be in a storm because you disobeyed. It's another thing to be in a storm because you did what you thought was right.

III. Jesus appears in the storm

   A. About four in the morning, Jesus came toward the disciples, walking on the water. "A ghost!" they cried out in terror. They didn't expect Jesus to come to them this way. Neither did you.

B. Jesus responds to their fear with an invitation that is worthy of inscription on every church cornerstone. "Courage. I AM. Fear not." He speaks courage into the storm. Not just calling for courage . . . releasing his supernatural courage.

C. The literal translation of Jesus' statement is "I AM." Jesus is not just announcing his presence on the sea but is announcing his *authority* over the sea. "I AM" has proclaimed his name over our problem as well. When we wonder, *Is anybody going to help me?* God says, "I AM."

IV. Courage comes from focusing on Christ

A. Peter understood who was commanding the weather. He would rather be out of the boat with Christ than in the boat without him. So when Jesus said, "Come, " Peter stepped out of the boat and walked on the water toward Jesus.

B. As long as Peter's focus was on Christ, he had courage. But the moment he looked somewhere else, he became afraid and he started to sink. The same is true in our lives.

C. Jesus extended his hand and pulled up a sinking Peter. Jesus likewise wants to get in the boat of your struggles. He knows that once you face him, you will have courage to face your problems.

SEA OF GALILEE

CAPERNAUM
SEA OF GALILEE

The area surrounding the Sea of Galilee has been populated since early times. Archaeological excavations have uncovered prehistoric tools and human remains, among the oldest recorded in the Middle East, and ancient Canaanite structures dating from 1000 to 2000 BC. The sea was located on the Via Maris, a Roman name for an ancient trade route dating back to the early Bronze Age that linked Egypt with the northern empires of Syria, Anatolia, and Mesopotamia.

The first-century historian Flavius Josephus (c. AD 37–100) was familiar with the region and wrote that "one may call this place the ambition of nature." He also documented a thriving industry along its shores, with some 230 boats regularly working in its waters. At least four of Jesus' disciples were fishermen on the Sea of Galilee: Simon (called Peter); Andrew, his brother; James, the son of Zebedee; and John, his brother. The Gospel of Mark reveals that Zebedee had "hired men" (1:20), which suggests that he had a thriving fishing enterprise.

The region gained special prominence for the Jewish people in AD 135 when the second Jewish revolt against the Romans, called the Bar Kokhba revolt, was put down. The Romans responded to the uprising by banning the Jews from Jerusalem, which led to the center of Jewish culture and learning shifting into the region (particularly to the city of Tiberias). By the fifth century AD, the region had become a major destination for Christian pilgrims.[6]

SIGNIFICANT EVENTS THAT TOOK PLACE ON OR NEAR THE SEA OF GALILEE	
Mary and Joseph settle twenty miles west of the sea	Matthew 2:19–23
Jesus calls Peter, Andrew, James, and John to follow him	Matthew 4:18–22
Jesus climbs a mountain near the sea and appoints the Twelve	Mark 3:13–19
Jesus crosses the sea to deliver a demon-possessed man	Mark 5:1–20
Jesus pays the temple tax from a fish caught in the sea	Matthew 17:24–27
Jesus feeds 4,000 people by the shores of the sea	Matthew 15:29–39
Jesus feeds 5,000 people by the shores of the sea	Luke 9:10–17
Jesus falls asleep while crossing the sea and then calms a storm	Mark 4:35–41
Jesus walks on the water of the sea in the midst of a storm	Matthew 14:22–27
Peter walks on the water of the sea but then starts to sink	Matthew 14:28–32
Jesus cooks breakfast for some of the disciples and restores Peter	John 21:1–25

Discuss | 35 MINUTES

Take some time to discuss what you just watched by answering the following questions. Use the suggested questions to begin your discussion, and then choose any of the additional questions as time allows.

Suggested Questions

1. Ask someone to read the story of Jesus walking on the water in Matthew 14:22–33. What was Jesus doing while the disciples were in the storm? Why do you think Jesus told the disciples to get in the boat ahead of him, knowing they would face a storm?

2. When the disciples saw Jesus walking on the water, they were terrified and thought he was a ghost. What did Jesus say to calm their fears? What is the literal rendering of his response—and what does that say about his power over the storm?

3. Peter took a bold step of faith by walking on the water toward Jesus, but he started to sink when he saw the wind. Jesus caught him and asked why he doubted (see verse 31). Why do you think we likewise tend to doubt Jesus' ability to calm our storms?

4. What impact did Jesus' miracle have on those who were in the boat that night (see verse 33)? Why is that significant?

Additional Questions

5. Jesus ordered the disciples to get into the boat and go to the other side of the Sea of Galilee. Has Jesus ever asked you do something that led you directly *into* a storm? If so, what happened, and how did it affect your faith?

6. What happened when Jesus got into the boat? Have you ever felt the presence of Christ in the middle of your storm? How did you know it was him?

7. Put yourself in the disciples' place. If you were on a boat, in a storm, and saw a figure walking on water, what would you think? How has Jesus approached you in unexpected ways, or in unexpected places, or through unexpected people?

8. Jesus revealed himself as the great I Am. The use of this name would have reassured the disciples of his power and reminded them of God's great deeds in the past. What are some of the ways that Jesus has revealed himself as the great I Am in your life?

Respond | 10 MINUTES

Review the outline for the video teaching and any notes you took. In the space below, write down your most significant takeaway from this session.

Pray | 10 MINUTES

End your time by praying together, asking the Lord to help you trust in him when you are in life's storms. Ask if anyone has any prayer requests. Write those requests in the space below so you and your group members can pray about them in the week ahead.

Name   Request

Personal Study

As you discussed in your group time this week, in this life you will encounter storms, but you can take courage because the great I Am promises to be with you in the midst of your trials. As you explore this theme in this week's personal study, be sure to write down your responses to the questions in the spaces provided, as you will be given a few minutes to share your insights at the start of the next session if you are doing this study with others. If you are reading *In the Footsteps of the Savior* alongside this study, first review chapter 5 in the book.

FINDING JESUS IN THE STORM

When Jesus appeared to the disciples on the boat, he was walking on water. Initially, this terrified the disciples: "'It's a ghost,' they said, and cried out in fear" (Matthew 14:26).

A belief in ghosts or spirits was common in antiquity. So it's little surprise that when the disciples saw someone doing something that humans can't do—like walk on water—they were convinced an apparition was walking toward them.[7] It was only after Jesus spoke that the disciples knew it was him (see verse 27). Even then, they were uncertain, so Peter asked for proof: "Lord, if it's you, tell me to come to you on the water" (verse 28).

It's easy to scoff at the disciples. How could they *not* have known it was Jesus? But how often have we missed Christ in our midst, especially when we're distracted by the storm around us? Jesus doesn't always show up the *way* that we think he will. He doesn't always show up *when* we think he will (remember the disciples had been battling the storm for hours before Jesus appeared). And he doesn't always *look* the way we think he will look. But that doesn't mean he doesn't come. It just means we have to be looking for him.

This is hard to do when we're anxious, stressed, or afraid of whatever the storm we're facing has brought into our lives. We're distracted by the fear and anxiety and fixated on what's going wrong. Even if Jesus is showing up, it's easy to miss him. But Jesus is the key to getting through the storm. If we lose sight of him or fail to trust in him, our storms will be that much more intense. But if we're aware of him and trust he is with us even as the waves rage, we can weather any storm. His presence brings us peace. His voice brings us hope.

READ | John 20:11–18

REFLECT

1. When Jesus was crucified, his followers were devastated. Their Savior was gone. They had seen him die. They had buried him. They were certain of his death. They had lost

all hope. But then, as we see in this passage, Jesus revealed himself to Mary. She had known him during his ministry. She was in the throes of grief after he died—a storm that many of us know all too well. Why do you think Mary didn't recognize Jesus at first?

2. Mary not only failed to recognize Jesus but also mistook him for the gardener who kept up the tombs. At what point *did* Mary recognize Jesus?

3. In the midst of Mary's sorrow, she heard Jesus' voice . . . and recognized it was him. Has it ever taken you a while to realize Jesus was with you in a storm or at another point in your life? What allowed you to finally recognize Jesus' presence with you?

4. What would it be like to hear Jesus speak your name in the midst of whatever storm you are facing? How would it change the way you feel about your storm?

PRAY | The Jesuit Prayer of Examen is a daily practice in which you are invited to examine the events of your day, give thanks, and note where you encountered God. For your prayer time today, go through these five steps of the prayer to help you notice where God met you today: (1) put yourself in God's presence; (2) pray for grace to see how God is working in your life; (3) go over events, conversations, and moments that stick out to you; (4) reflect on these events, conversations, and moments, and (5) ask God to help you be aware of his presence tomorrow.[8]

WHAT STORMS REVEAL

It's one thing to encounter a storm when you've done something wrong. Your behavior or choices led you to the consequences you are now reaping. But it's another thing to encounter a storm after doing *exactly* what God told you to do. Why would he lead you this way when he knew you would encounter darkness, sickness, or death? Why did he tell you to make that move, take that job, or start a family when he knew the heartache that would follow?

The disciples were likely wondering this as well that stormy night. Jesus was the one who told them to cross the sea: "Immediately Jesus made the disciples get into the boat and go on ahead of him to the other side" (Matthew 14:22). While Jesus prayed on the mountain, they were hit with wave after wave. They must have wondered why Jesus told them to cross the sea.

It's natural during storms to ask the *why* question. *Why did this happen? Why am I having to endure this trial? Why did God tell me to go this way?* But there's something interesting to note about the story. After Jesus climbed into the boat and the waves died down, we read, "Those who were in the boat worshiped him, saying, 'Truly you are the Son of God'" (verse 33). This is the first account in Matthew of the disciples worshiping Jesus. They had felt in awe of him and were amazed by him (see 8:27), but they had not worshiped him until now. They were finally seeing him for who he truly was: their God who was worthy of worship.

It's hard to know the purpose of our storms when we are right in the middle of them. But in each one, Jesus is telling us something about himself—revealing more of who he is to us—so that in the next storm we will know who is there with us: the Son of God, who is worthy of our worship.

READ | John 1:1–14

REFLECT

1. John opens his Gospel with this "great prologue" that describes how Jesus chose to take on human flesh and dwell among us. (Note that the term *Word* in this passage

refers to Christ.) What does John say about who Jesus was, is, and always will be (see verses 1–5)?

2, John goes on to state that Jesus is "the true light that gives light to everyone" (verse 9). Yet some did not recognize that light and chose instead to live in darkness. But what promise is given for those who do choose to "believe in his name" (verse 12)?

3, Think about a storm you have been through that made you ask the *why* question. How has God illuminated his purposes in having you go through that trial? What new truths did you learn about God and yourself after going through that storm?

4, The disciples' *why* questions melted away when they recognized *who* was with them in the storm. In what ways do you need God to reveal his presence to you today?

PRAY | Read through John 1:1–14 for your prayer time today. Underline whatever stands out to you about Jesus' character. Meditate on those descriptions of Christ.

— Day 3 —

KEEPING YOUR FOCUS

We live in a world where at any given moment a dozen different distractions are demanding our attention: phones, email, YouTube, podcasts, news, audiobooks, and the like. With all these distractions, it can be difficult to find a moment of quiet in our day. What's more, when we are in a trying situation in our lives, it's all too easy to turn to these distractions . . . either for help, or guidance, or to numb our emotions or put off dealing with what is right in front of us.

In this week's story, we saw that Peter made a bold request of Jesus: "Lord, if it's you . . . tell me to come to you on the water" (Matthew 14:28). Jesus told him to come, and Peter obeyed and stepped over the side. In so doing, Peter accomplished what no other person in Scripture had done before, not even the great prophets like Elijah: *he walked on water.*[9]

Peter was partaking in a miracle of Jesus! But then he heard and felt the wind howling around him. He was reminded that he was in the midst of a raging storm. He saw that the waves were big . . . much bigger than he was. He forgot that Jesus was *bigger*.

It can be difficult for us to keep our focus on Christ in the midst of a storm. We're battling the waves around us. We're paddling desperately to get to the other side. We're trying to navigate the anxiety, fear, and all the other emotions that we are experiencing. It all seems so *big,* and we forget that Christ is bigger. He is greater than the storm. He is the I AM. He is our courage, our strength, our hope, and our peace. All we have to do is put down the phone, take our eyes off the anxiety for a moment, and look up at him. For just like he did with Peter, he is offering us his hand.

READ | Hebrews 12:1–3

REFLECT

1. In Hebrews 11, the chapter before this passage, the author provides a detailed history of the heroes of the Jewish faith who followed God wherever he led them: Abraham, Sarah, Isaac, and Joseph, to name a few. The author's point is that because of these

great examples who've gone before us, we can do the same when we focus on Christ. According to verse 1, what should we throw off so we can run the race of faith?

2, What do you think it means for Jesus to be the pioneer and perfecter of our faith?

3, What tends to distract you from focusing on Jesus, especially during trying times?

4, Think about something you're worried about today. How could you instead focus on Jesus? How could you "throw off" whatever is keeping you from focusing on him?

PRAY | End your time in prayer. Ask Jesus to forgive you for being so easily distracted from him. Ask him to help you look to him—and only him—to calm your fears and anxieties. Thank him for reaching out his hand to you and pulling you up when it feels like you're sinking.

PEACE IN THE STORM

As soon as Jesus stepped onto the boat, "the wind died down" (Matthew 14:32). This isn't the only time in Scripture that Jesus calmed a storm. In the Gospel of Mark, the disciples and Jesus found themselves in another storm on the Sea of Galilee. The disciples begged Jesus for help. As a result, "[Jesus] got up, rebuked the wind and said to the waves, 'Quiet! Be still!' Then the wind died down and it was completely calm" (4:39).

Sometimes, this is what Jesus does with our storms. He brings miraculous peace, healing, and restoration. All is resolved. But more often, the peace that Jesus offers does not *end* our storms. Instead, he offers us peace *during* the storm and *in spite of* the storm. The problem persists, the illness lingers, the situation remains unresolved. But this doesn't mean Jesus isn't there. In him, we can have inner peace even when our outer world is dark and stormy.

We often look for peace in places we can never find it. We think that if we just had more money, or had different friends, or were just in a different place in life, *then* all the unsettledness that we feel inside would go away. But what happens when those problems are finally solved? Another one just pops up in its place, and we are no better off than we were before.

What we need is the peace of God. The kind of peace that God offers is not a mere solution to a problem nor an offer of worldly contentment. Rather, the peace that God offers is *an ongoing state of mind.* An undercurrent to our turbulent lives. A voice saying that no matter what is happening on the outside, we can have peace on the inside.

READ | John 14:25–27

REFLECT

1. Jesus tried to explain to his followers that he wouldn't be with them forever and that he would one day be reunited with his Father in heaven. This troubled the disciples, who couldn't understand when or how Jesus would do this. They wanted

their rabbi and friend to stay with them. So Jesus reassured them. How did he do this? What did Jesus promise the disciples would receive once he had left the earth?

2. What does Jesus reveal about the Holy Spirit? What are some of the gifts he would provide to the disciples—and to us?

3. When you feel unsettled, whether due to a storm in your life or discontentment, to whom or what do you tend to turn to find peace? What has been the result?

4. Jesus told his disciples, "Do not let your hearts be troubled and do not be afraid" (verse 27). What is troubling your heart today? What peace do you need from the Holy Spirit?

PRAY | In your prayer time today, ask Jesus for his peace—not the peace the world offers, but the peace that only he can offer. Sit and wait in silence for a few minutes. Allow Jesus' peace to wash over you. Note how you feel after this time of prayer and meditation.

Day 5

CATCH UP AND REFLECT

Use this time to go back and complete any study and reflection questions from previous days this week that you weren't able to finish. Make a note below of any revelations you've had and reflect on any growth or personal insights you've gained.

Spend the next two days reading chapter 4 of *In the Footsteps of the Savior*. Use the space below to record anything in the chapters that stands out to you or encourages you.

WEEK 3

BEFORE GROUP MEETING	Read chapter 4 of *In the Footsteps of the Savior* Read the Welcome section (page 49)
GROUP MEETING	Discuss the Connect questions Watch the video teaching for session 3 Discuss the questions that follow as a group Do the closing exercise and pray (pages 50–58)
PERSONAL STUDY – DAY 1	Complete the daily study (pages 60–61)
PERSONAL STUDY – DAY 2	Complete the daily study (pages 62–63)
PERSONAL STUDY – DAY 3	Complete the daily study (pages 64–64)
PERSONAL STUDY – DAY 4	Complete the daily study (pages 66–68)
PERSONAL STUDY – DAY 5 (before week 4 group meeting)	Complete the daily study (page 69) Read chapter 8 of *In the Footsteps of the Savior* Complete any unfinished personal studies

MOUNT OF BEATITUDES

FOLLOWING JESUS WHEN YOU WORRY

"So do not worry, saying, 'What shall we eat?' or 'What shall we drink?' or 'What shall we wear?' For the pagans run after all these things, and your heavenly Father knows that you need them. But seek first his kingdom and his righteousness, and all these things will be given to you."

MATTHEW 6:31-33

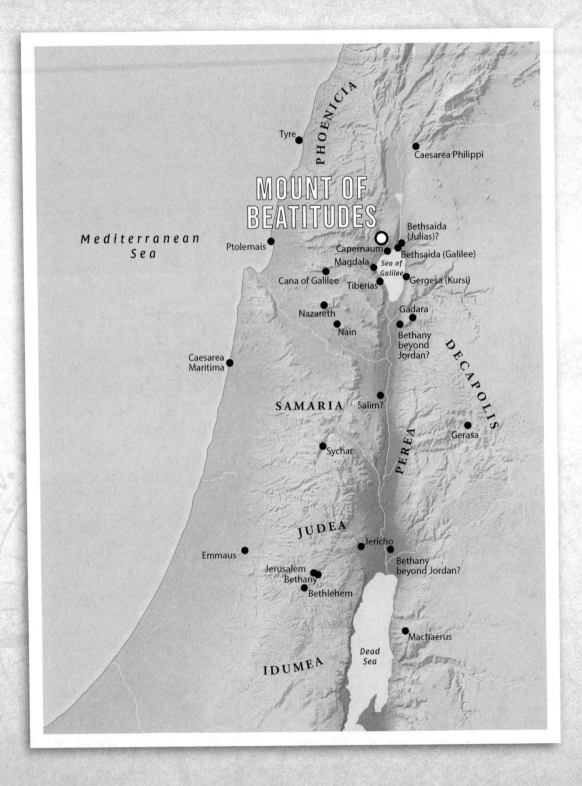

Welcome | READ ON YOUR OWN

What is your relationship with worry? Is it a constant companion? An unwelcome guest who overstays its visit? A friend from the past who now only shows up occasionally? No matter how often or intensely you feel worry, you are not immune to its presence and the effects it has on you, your mood, your health, and your relationships. Worry wreaks havoc.

The people of Jesus' day certainly had many reasons to worry. Poverty was a constant threat. Natural disasters could be devastating. Tensions were typically high between the Jews and the Romans who occupied the land. Yes, the people had many *good* reasons to be concerned about their lives. Yet Jesus still commanded them, "Do not worry" (Matthew 6:25).

As you will see in this session, Jesus spoke these words in what we call the Sermon on the Mount. Many believe the setting for this famous message was the Mount of Beatitudes, a hill in northern Israel that overlooks a beautiful and lush landscape. It would have been the perfect place for Jesus to point out the flowers in the fields below and call the people's attention to the birds in the air . . . and remind them that they can trust God to care for them.

Worry hasn't gone away since Jesus' time. In fact, there is evidence that people are more worried now than ever before.[10] But just as worry has remained, so has Jesus—and the words he spoke on the Mount of Beatitudes apply just as readily to our lives today.

Connect | 15 MINUTES

Get the session started by choosing one of the following questions to discuss as a group:

- What is a key insight or takeaway from last week's personal study that you would like to share with the group?

  — or —

- How would you describe what your relationship is like with worry?

Watch | 20 MINUTES

Now watch the video for this session. As you watch, use the following outline to record any thoughts or concepts that stand out to you.

I. The nature of worry in our lives

A. Regardless of what age you are, the questions fall like hailstones. *Will I make enough money? Will I make any friends? Will I have a cubicle? Will I be able to learn the software program?*

B. What does all this anxiety mean? Simply this: you are a human being.

C. Jesus battled anxiety in the Garden of Gethsemane. His heart pumped with such ferocity that capillaries broke and rivulets of crimson streaked his face.

II. Jesus' words on worry

    A. Jesus didn't stay anxious. He entrusted his fears to his heavenly Father and completed his earthly mission with faith. He will help us to do likewise.

    B. The largest section of the Sermon on the Mount encompasses Jesus' words on worry. It is relevant to the day and age in which we live. It's hard to miss the theme of these verses:

        1. "I tell you not to worry about everyday life" (Matthew 6:25 NLT).

        2. "Can all your worries add a single moment to your life?" (verse 27 NLT).

        3. "Why worry . . . ?" (verse 28, NLT)

4. "So don't worry about these things . . ." (verse 31 NLT).

5. "Don't worry . . . " (verse 34 NLT).

C. Worry simply does not work. We can dedicate a decade of worry and anxious thoughts to our lives and not grow one inch. Worry accomplishes nothing. But still . . . we worry.

III. What to do with our worry

A. Jesus, and later the apostle Paul, never condemn legitimate and healthy concerns. Rather, they speak of a continuous mindset of worry that dismisses God's presence. "Therefore I tell you, stop being perpetually uneasy (anxious and worried) about your life" (Matthew 6:25 AMPC).

B. The call not to worry is a call to avoid a *state of mind* in which God is disregarded and even distrusted. It's a call to not have an outlook on life that subtracts God from the future and faces uncertainties with no faith and no hope. It's a call to put God into the equation.

C. The moment you feel anxious, you can take your thoughts to God. You could lie in bed and stress about the day ahead, or you could climb out of bed and say, "Thank you, Lord, you have been good to me." Turn every fret into a prayer, and you'll be praying all the time.

IV. Eight worry stoppers

A. Keep a worry diary. Over a period of days, record your anxious thoughts that trouble you. Then review them and ask the question, "How many of them became a reality?"

B. Evaluate your worry categories. You have a thematic type of worry. For every fruit, there is a root! So evaluate your category, and once you find that theme, talk to Jesus about it.

C. **Take your worries to Christ.** At the wedding in Cana, when the hosts ran out of wine, the first thing Mary did was to go to Jesus with the problem. See how quickly you can do the same.

D. **Leave your worries with Christ.** "Casting the whole of your care . . . on Him" (1 Peter 5:7 AMPC).

E. **Recruit a worry army.** Jesus took three prayer warriors into the Garden of Gethsemane with him. If he took three prayer warriors with him, how much more should we?

F. **Become a worry slapper.** Treat frets like mosquitoes. The moment a concern surfaces, deal with it. Don't assume worry is a part of life.

G. **Understand God's manna plan.** God meets needs daily. You'll have what you need tomorrow when tomorrow comes. For now, you have enough for today, and that's enough.

H. **Let God be enough.** "Seek first the kingdom of God and His righteousness" (Matthew 6:33 NKJV). Worry disappears as we seek God's kingdom.

MOUNT OF BEATITUDES

Like most places listed in the New Testament, we do not know the exact location of the Mount of Beatitudes. However, during the fourth century AD, Christian pilgrims began traveling to a small hillside that overlooks the Sea of Galilee where they believed Jesus gave the sermon. A church was built there in the late fourth century AD, the ruins of which can still be seen today. The hillside, once known as Mount Eremos, is located between the village of Capernaum and what Josephus called the "well of Capernaum," a popular fishing spot in the first century (now called Tabgha) where it believed several episodes in Jesus' ministry took place.

Today the hillside is topped by structure that is appropriately called the Church of the Beatitudes. The church was built in the Neo-Byzantine style between 1936 to 1936 with the support of the Italian dictator Mussolini. Designed by noted architect Antonio Barluzzi, it features an octagonal floor plan, with the eight different sides of the church representing the eight Beatitudes. Outside, in front of the church, are symbols on the pavement representing the qualities of justice, prudence, fortitude, charity, faith, and temperance.[11]

KEY SECTIONS OF THE SERMON ON THE MOUNT	
The Beatitudes	Matthew 5:3–11
Salt and light	Matthew 5:13–16
Jesus is the fulfillment of the law	Matthew 5:17–20
Teachings on murder, adultery, divorce, and oaths	Matthew 5:21–37
Loving your enemies	Matthew 5:38–48
Giving to the needy	Matthew 6:1–4
Teachings on prayer and fasting	Matthew 6:5–18
Treasures in heaven	Matthew 6:19–24
Do not worry	Matthew 6:25–25
Judging others	Matthew 7:1–6
Seeking God and the wide and narrow gates	Matthew 7:7–13
True and false prophets and disciples	Matthew 7:15–23
The wise and foolish builders	Matthew 7:24–27

Discuss | 35 MINUTES

Take some time to discuss what you just watched by answering the following questions. Use the suggested questions to begin your discussion, and then choose any of the additional questions as time allows.

Suggested Questions

1. What do you believe about anxiety? Do you believe it's sinful, normal, a sign you're lacking in faith? From where did your thoughts about anxiety originate?

2. What is the difference between worry and legitimate and healthy concerns? What are some examples of healthy concerns that you have right now in your life? What are some examples of concerns you have that have turned into worries?

3. Take a moment to review Jesus' words in Matthew 6:25–34. What kind of worries did Jesus talk about in this passage? Why should we not worry? What does this tell you about how God feels about us and the details of our lives?

4. Read Philippians 4:6. What does Paul advise us to do with our worries? What role does thanksgiving, or gratitude, play when it comes to our worries?

Additional Questions

5. Review the eight worry-stoppers. Which of these have you used before to help combat worry? Which ones would be useful to help with your current anxieties?

6. Ask someone in the group to read Exodus 16:1–4 and 17–20. Why do you think God commanded the Israelites to gather just enough manna for the day? Why do you think some disregarded this command? Why is it hard to trust God with our daily needs?

7. Ask someone to reread Matthew 6:33–34. Why does seeking God first help to alleviate our worries? What is an example from your life when you've sought something other than God first? What kind of anxieties arose as a result?

8. What keeps you from bringing certain worries to Christ? What do you need to believe about him today in order to bring *all* of your worries to him?

Respond | 10 MINUTES

Review the outline for the video teaching and any notes you took. In the space below, write down your most significant takeaway from this session.

Pray | 10 MINUTES

End your time by praying together as a group, asking the Lord to help you commit all your worries to him. Ask if anyone has any prayer requests to share. Write those requests down in the space below so you and your group members can pray about them in the week ahead.

Name	Request

Personal Study

As you discussed in your group time this week, worries come with life . . . but they don't have to control our lives. We can take our worries to Christ each day and trust that he will provide for us each day. As you explore this theme in this week's personal study, write down your responses to the questions in the spaces provided, as you will be given a few minutes to share your insights at the start of the next session if you are doing this study with others. If you are reading *In the Footsteps of the Savior* alongside this study, first review chapter 4 in the book.

OUR GREAT EMPATHIZER

Anxiety and other mental health issues are often stigmatized in our culture and in the church. Perhaps you've encountered some who will urge you to just pray away your struggles. Some may have judged you for not having enough faith because you're struggling with an anxiety disorder. But as you learned in this week's session, experiencing anxiety—even chronic and debilitating anxiety—doesn't make you a failure, and it doesn't mean you're not a Christian.

Jesus urged us not to worry, but that's not because he never worried himself. The Gospels reveal that he *did* worry. On the night before his crucifixion, we are told that he was in so much anguish over the events to come that "his sweat was like drops of blood" (Luke 22:44). Some have linked this description to a rare condition known as hematohidrosis, in which severe anxiety or depression can cause someone to secrete blood.[12]

So, not only did Jesus experience anxiety, but he also experienced it at the deepest and most intense level. This is the beautiful thing about Christ: he felt what we feel and experienced what we experience. This is why he could tell us not to worry about our lives—not because it was sinful to do so but because he knew what worry felt like. He knew how consuming it could be. He gave this instruction from a place of empathy, not condemnation.

Perhaps you have been judged for having an anxiety disorder or feeling crippled by your anxiety. Perhaps you have judged others for these same things. Anxiety and worry are unavoidable. These feelings are often upon us before we can stop them. But in Christ, we have a great empathizer for this type of pain. We have someone who knows exactly what it feels like, and because of this we can be sure we are never alone, even in our deepest anxiety.

READ | Luke 22:39–44

REFLECT

1. The cup that Jesus refers to in this passage is a likely a reference to the cup of judgment mentioned in Scripture (see Psalm 75:7-8). Jesus knew he was about to receive

the harshest judgment—the sins of the world—which would lead to him receiving the harshest punishment: crucifixion. How is Jesus' anxiety described in this passage?

2. What did Jesus do even after the angel appeared to him to strengthen him? What does this say about how worried he felt in that moment?

3. Think of a time you felt intense anxiety—a type of worry that has kept you up at night. What caused it? What did it feel like in your body and in your mind?

4. How does it feel to know that Jesus has felt that way too? How could this change the way you approach Jesus the next time you are in the throes of anxiety?

PRAY | Bring your worries before the Lord in prayer. Remember that Jesus has felt the way you feel. You can be honest with him. He isn't afraid of what you are feeling or what you are facing.

— Day 2 —

JUST GO TO GOD

How many times have you gone through your day worrying about something? You come up with every worst-case scenario. You plan for multiple outcomes and stress out about each one. When you get in bed at night, you're still worried. You are still ruminating on the thing causing your anxiety. At any point in your day, did you pause and ask God to help you?

This is what Paul urges us to do in Philippians 4:6: "Do not be anxious about anything, but in every situation, by prayer and petition, with thanksgiving, present your requests to God." By prayer and petition, we are to make our requests known to God in *every situation*. Some situations are beyond human help and understanding, but no situation is beyond divine intervention. When we are worried, all we have to do is ask God for what we need.

We can be specific in our requests. *God, the brakes on my car went out, and I don't have the money to fix it . . . please help. God, I'm going to college and I don't know anybody . . . please give me a friend. God, I am sick and don't know what to do next . . . point me to a kind, compassionate, and capable doctor.*

This is exactly what Mary, the mother of Jesus, did at the wedding at Cana. The host of the wedding had run out of wine. Now, we might be tempted to disregard this as not a big deal. After all, they had water to drink, and no one was going to go thirsty. But weddings in Jesus' time lasted for *seven days*. The bride and groom had invited as many people as possible, and they were expected to provide enough wine to last all seven days for every guest. If they ran it out, it was considered a major social faux pas that the community would never forget.[13]

Mary was trying to protect this family from humiliation. The stakes were high. But instead of panicking, she asked Jesus to help, and she trusted that he could.

READ | John 2:1-11

REFLECT

1. This was Jesus' first public miracle, as evidenced by the fact that he told his mother, "Why do you involve me? . . . My hour has not yet come" (verse 4). We don't know if

Mary had seen him perform other miracles, but it's clear that Jesus had not gone to this wedding intending to perform one there. Still, Mary seemed to know that Jesus could and *would* fix the problem. Why do you think she believed in him?

2. Look at the way Jesus fixed the problem. He went above and beyond what was needed to solve the crisis. What does tell you about how he is able to work in your life?

3. Take a moment to make a list of some of the things that are causing you anxiety right now. Have you asked Jesus for what you need? Why or why not?

4. Use your imagination for a moment. What are some ways that Jesus could provide for you above and beyond in this anxiety-inducing situation?

PRAY | Spend your prayer time asking Jesus for *exactly* what you need in this situation. Be specific and believe that he will come thorough and provide whatever you need.

Faith and Anxiety

We feel anxiety about our physical lives. We worry about money, health, food, and shelter. We feel anxiety about our emotional lives. We worry about friendships, relationships, and finding love. But there are also times when we feel anxiety about our spiritual lives. For some of us, our faith can actually be the cause of our anxiety. We worry if we are doing enough. We worry about past sin. We worry about salvation. We worry that we're not enough, even for God.

Spiritual anxiety can be some of the most intense kinds of anxiety. We're guessing at what God wants us to do, always unsure and always afraid that we will take the wrong step or make the wrong move. The fear of suffering for eternity, the fear of falling short of God's love, the fear that we've gone too far to be redeemed . . . this can cause anxiety for a lifetime.

Jesus did not spread a message of needing to be enough or do enough. In fact, his words to his followers were just the opposite. As the apostle Paul would later write, "For all have sinned and fall short of the glory of God, *and* all are justified freely by his grace through the redemption that came by Christ Jesus" (Romans 23-24, emphasis added). Don't forget the *and*.

When we have spiritual anxiety, it's because we're focusing on the "fallen short" part. We *have* sinned. But in Christ, that's not the end of the story. The end of the story is this: we are all "justified freely by his grace." The justification is free. There's nothing we can do to earn it. We *aren't* enough, but that's okay, because Jesus is enough. Anxiety caused by faith is not of God because he did not send his Son to spread a message of fear. He sent his Son to set us free.

READ | Romans 8:31–39

Reflect

1. Paul had established many churches in the Mediterranean region, but evidently not the ones in Rome. He was planning on visiting the Christians there on his way to taking the gospel to Spain, and it is likely he wrote this letter in advance of that trip to outline his presentation of the gospel. He wanted the believers in Rome to understand God's grace and that he was *for* them. How can you likewise know that God is for you?

2. Paul writes that God did not spare even the life of his own Son when it came to his plan for salvation. What does Paul conclude in this about the love of God? How does this prove his point that there is absolutely *nothing* that can separate us from God's love?

3. What kind of anxiety about your faith have you experienced in the past? What kind of spiritual anxiety do you feel today?

4. What have you believed could separate you from God's love? Why did you believe this? How does this passage give you hope in the face of that belief today?

PRAY | Spend your prayer time declaring Romans 8:37–39. Declare that nothing can separate you from God's love. Challenge any anxiety you've felt over that possibility with this passage.

FEAR OF THE FUTURE

While life offers us plenty of reasons to worry and feel anxious, perhaps nothing creates more anxiety for us than an unknown future. The unknown just makes us uncomfortable. We feel out of control when we don't know what's next or can't imagine the next step.

Maybe at some point you felt certain about your future and where you were headed, but then something happened that pulled the rug out from under your plans. Maybe you now have a big decision to make, and you want to make the right one, but there's no crystal ball before you and you don't know how to decide. Everyone faces an unknown future. You might think you know what is coming . . . but the reality is that no one really does.

The disciples felt this way. Jesus tried to tell them about his future. He tried to tell them that he would be leaving them one day. But they didn't understand. They didn't want to lose their friend. They didn't know where he was going, even when he tried to explain it to them. And they felt anxiety as a result. Where was Christ going? What would they do without him?

Even though they were uncertain, Jesus was not. He knew where he was going, and he knew the disciples would be reunited with him one day. He knows this about our future as well. He knows where we are headed. He knows that we will be reunited with him one day.

It's not our job to know every step of our own journeys. It's our job to trust that Jesus does know the way. He knows the plans that he has for us. He knows that we will ultimately be in his Father's house with him. He knows all this because he has prepared a place for us there.

READ | John 13:33–14:3

REFLECT

1. Jesus spoke these words to his disciples as they shared the Passover meal together the night before his crucifixion. When he said, "I will be with you only a little longer"

(verse 33), he knew that in just a few short hours events would start to unfold that would lead to his death—and change the disciples' futures forever. Think about Peter's response to Jesus' words. How do you think he felt hearing Jesus say this?

2. What assurances does Jesus offer in this passage? List or underline each one.

What questions do you have for Jesus about your future?

 Which of the assurances in this passage do you need most today? Why?

PRAY | Jesus said, "I will come back and take you to be with me that you also may be where I am" (verse 3). Jesus' presence is peace and comfort. So, during your prayer time today, enter into Jesus' presence. Sit with him. Let him whisper words of peace and comfort over you.

Day 5

CATCH UP AND REFLECT

Use this time to go back and complete any study and reflection questions from previous days this week that you weren't able to finish. Make a note below of any revelations you've had and reflect on any growth or personal insights you've gained.

Spend the next two days reading chapter 8 of *In the Footsteps of the Savior*. Use the space below to record anything in the chapters that stands out to you or encourages you.

WEEK 4

BEFORE GROUP MEETING	Read chapter 8 of *In the Footsteps of the Savior* Read the Welcome section (page 73)
GROUP MEETING	Discuss the Connect questions Watch the video teaching for session 4 Discuss the questions that follow as a group Do the closing exercise and pray (pages 74–82)
PERSONAL STUDY – DAY 1	Complete the daily study (pages 84–85)
PERSONAL STUDY – DAY 2	Complete the daily study (pages 86–87)
PERSONAL STUDY – DAY 3	Complete the daily study (pages 88–89)
PERSONAL STUDY – DAY 4	Complete the daily study (pages 90–92)
PERSONAL STUDY – DAY 5 (before week 5 group meeting)	Complete the daily study (page 93) Read chapters 9–10 of *In the Footsteps of the Savior* Complete any unfinished personal studies

TEMPLE STEPS

FOLLOWING JESUS . . . AND ONLY JESUS

"The words I say to you I do not speak on my own authority. Rather, it is the Father, living in me, who is doing his work. Believe me when I say that I am in the Father and the Father is in me; or at least believe on the evidence of the works themselves."

JOHN 14:10-11

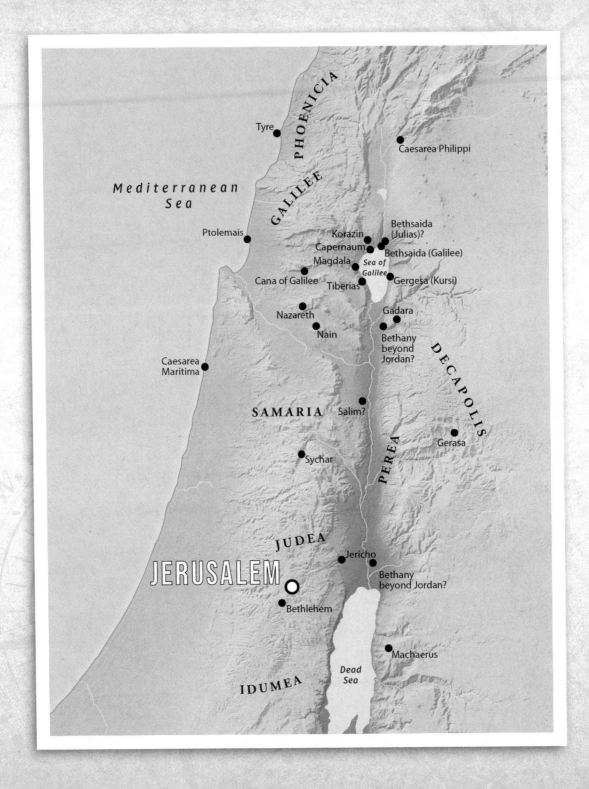

Welcome | READ ON YOUR OWN

The Southern Steps lead up to the Southern Wall of Jerusalem. In Jesus' time, these would have been the steps that he and other pilgrims took to get to the Temple. It was common for rabbis to teach on these steps, spreading their messages of God and the Messiah.[14]

During Jesus' time, there were others spreading the message that they were the Messiah or knew the Messiah. Jesus wasn't the only one making this claim . . . just as he isn't the only one making it today. Today, the "saviors" we follow are a bit different. They take the form of money, fame, popularity, and power, among others. Just like the people in Jesus' day, we have to be careful not to look to anything for our salvation except Christ.

In this session, you will read about a Pharisee named Nicodemus, who visited Jesus at night. Nicodemus wanted to know what this rabbi from Nazareth was all about. Jesus responded by telling him that he was the *one and only* . . . the one and only Messiah, the one and only Savior, the one and only Son of God. "For God so loved the world that he gave his one and only Son, that whoever believes in him shall not perish but have eternal life" (John 3:16).

Nicodemus had a hard time believing this. So do we. If we didn't, we wouldn't chase all the things we hope will fulfill us and give us the life we desire. We wouldn't ignore the fact that Jesus already came to give us that life. One free of burdens, sin, striving, and pain. Jesus came to set us free—and he is the one and only who can.

Connect | 15 MINUTES

Get the session started by choosing one of the following questions to discuss as a group:

- What is a key insight or takeaway from last week's personal study that you would like to share with the group?

— *or* —

- What are some of the things in this world that people turn to for salvation?

Watch | 20 MINUTES

Now watch the video for this session. As you watch, use the following outline to record any thoughts or concepts that stand out to you.

I. The uniqueness of Jesus Christ

    A. We do not believe that our lives are just a brief trip between a birth and the hearse. We believe that we are here to make a decision—and that is what to do with Jesus Christ.

    B. Jesus is unlike any other of the billions of human beings that have ever lived. He made claims that either make him the hope or the hoax of mankind. He made claims that set him apart.

    C. "For God so loved the world that he gave his one and only Son, that whoever believes in him shall not perish but have eternal life" (John 3:16). At the heart of that verse is the heart of the claims of Jesus Christ. He claimed to be the only and only Son of God.

II. Jesus' one and only relationship with the Father

    A. The Greek work *monogenes* highlights the singular relationship that Jesus had with God the Father. We are all children of God but none of us in a *monogenetic* child of God.

    B. Only Christ can be called the *monogenetic* Son of God because only he has the genetic makeup of God. Just as our children have our genetic makeup, so Jesus carries God's DNA .

    C. Jesus enjoys a relationship with God that is unprecedented and unexperienced by anyone in human history. He claims to enjoy the Christ the Redeemer perch high above all.

III. Jesus is the one and only ruler and revealer

    A. Matthew gives us more details about what this means in his Gospel: "My Father has given me authority over everything" (Matthew 11:27 NLT). Jesus claims to be the one and only ruler over everything.

        1. A Roman officer sent a message to Jesus, asking him to come and heal his servant (see Luke 7:1–10). Before Jesus arrived, the master sent a servant to tell Jesus, "It's an unnecessary trip. Just say the word where you are and my servant will be healed."

        2. The officer was part of the Roman Empire and understood authority. He was saying, "I get authority, and Jesus, you have authority. You call the shots."

        3. Jesus replied, "I tell you the truth, I haven't seen faith like this in all Israel!" (Matthew 8:10 NLT). Jesus did not correct the officer but applauded him and said, "Okay, here is faith."

B. Jesus is the one and only revealer. "No one truly knows the Son except the Father, and no one truly knows the Father except the Son" (Matthew 11:27 NLT). Nobody knows God except Jesus.

C. Jesus says that he shares an intimacy with God. Consequently, when he speaks, he speaks with God's authority. Jesus claims to be not a *top* theologian, not an *accomplished* theologian, not even the *supreme* theologian. He claims to be the *only* theologian.

IV. Jesus' invitation as the one and only Son of God

A. Jesus is the only theologian to ever live. He has walked pedestrian streets that no other human being has walked and has witnessed moments that no other person ever will.

B. Jesus doesn't just boast in his knowledge; he shares it. He doesn't just gloat; he gives. He doesn't just revel; he reveals. He reveals to us the secrets of eternity. We don't understand them all, but we can ask and we can seek them. He shares them freely.

C. Accept Jesus' invitation and let him teach you. He can handle any problem you have. He knows the right choice about every decision you make. Don't go to others. Go to him.

D. Seek him out. Don't stop searching until you find him. Lift up your eyes and set your sights on him. No passing glances or occasional glimpses. Make Jesus your point of reference.

TEMPLE STEPS

JERUSALEM

All that remains today of the Temple that existed in Jesus' day is a portion of the original retaining wall (called the Wailing Wall) and a series of steps that led up to the Temple from the south. The Temple Steps, as they are known, were unearthed by archaeologists in 1967 and were part of a pilgrim's road that led from the Pool of Siloam to the Temple Mount. It is believed that Jesus and the disciples would have used these steps in their day.

The First Temple was built during the reign of King Solomon in 957 BC. However, this structure was destroyed in 587 BC when the Babylonians invaded the kingdom of Judah, conquered its people, and took them into exile. When the Persians then conquered the Babylonians in 539 BC, the people of Judah were allowed to return to their homeland in waves, starting one year later in 538 BC. These returning exiles began work on constructing the Second Temple . . . but by all accounts it was a modest structure and nothing like the first.

But then in 20 BC, a Roman-Jewish client king named Herod took up the project. Herod began with a massive expansion of the Temple Mount, enlarging its area from 17 to 36 acres. He brought in architects from Greece, Rome, and Egypt to craft the Second Temple into an impressive an awe-inspiring structure. Main work on the Temple was completed in just one and a half years, but renovations continued to be made until AD 63. Herod's Temple, as it became known, lasted until AD 70, when the Romans laid siege to Jerusalem and destroyed it.[15]

SIGNIFICANT EVENTS THAT TOOK PLACE IN THE TEMPLE	
Jesus is presented as a child in the Temple	Luke 2:22–24
Mary and Joseph find Jesus at age twelve in the Temple	Luke 2:42–46
Satan takes Jesus to the highest point of the Temple	Matthew 4:5
Jesus cleanses the Temple the first time	John 2:13–16
Jesus teaches in the Temple at the Feast of Tabernacles	John 7:14
A woman caught in adultery is brought to Jesus at the Temple	John 8:2–6
Jesus cleanses the Temple the second time	Mark 11:15–17
Jesus teaches in the Temple as the Jewish leaders plot to kill him	Luke 19:47
Jesus heals the blind and the lame in the Temple	Matthew 21:14
People in the Temple cry out to Jesus in praise	Matthew 21:15
The veil in the Temple is torn at Jesus' death	Matthew 27:50–51

Discuss | 35 MINUTES

Take some time to discuss what you just watched by answering the following questions. Use the suggested questions to begin your discussion, and then choose any of the additional questions as time allows.

Suggested Questions

1. When did you first encounter Christ? How did he change your path or direction?

2. Ask someone to read John 3:16. What Greek word is translated *one and only*? What is the significance of this word? What does it tell us about Jesus' relationship to God?

3. Review Luke 7:1–10. How did the centurion show faith in Jesus? How did Jesus react to the centurion's faith? What does it mean to have faith in Jesus' authority in this way?

4. Ask someone to read aloud Matthew 11:27. How is Jesus our revealer? What does he reveal? What specific revelation do you need from Jesus today?

Additional Questions

5. What is your closest relationship—a person you could represent or speak on behalf of because you know him or her so well? How does this type of relationship you have with that person help you understand the relationship between Jesus and the Father?

6. Ask someone in the group to read aloud Matthew 11:28. Why does Jesus say that he is able to teach us? What will happen if we allow him to teach us?

7. What has Christ taught you? How did he teach this to you?

8. Jesus is the one and only authority and revealer. Which of these characteristics of Christ is the most difficult for you to understand? Why?

Respond | 10 MINUTES

Review the outline for the video teaching and any notes you took. In the space below, write down your most significant takeaway from this session.

Pray | 10 MINUTES

End your time by praying together as a group, thanking the Lord for sending his one and only Son into this world. Ask if anyone has any prayer requests to share. Write those requests down in the space below so you and your group members can pray about them in the week ahead.

Name   Request

Personal Study

As you discussed in your group time this week, Jesus didn't just claim to be a top theologian, or an accomplished theologian, or even a supreme theologian. He claimed to be the *only* theologian. He alone knows the Father . . . and he has chosen to reveal the secrets of eternity to us. As you explore this theme in this week's personal study, write down your responses to the questions in the spaces provided, as you will be given a few minutes to share your insights at the start of the next session if you are doing this study with others. If you are reading *In the Footsteps of the Savior* alongside this study, first review chapter 8 in the book.

-Day 1-

THE CORNERSTONE

In the architecture of Jesus' day, a cornerstone was the most crucial element of a structure. The cornerstone was used to adjoin two walls together. It was much larger than the other stones used in the construction, as it had to serve as a firm foundation for the entire building. The cornerstone was also smoother than the other stones, so it was often used for inscriptions denoting who constructed the building—such as the architect or the king who funded it.[16]

A cornerstone is often employed in Scripture as a symbol for Christ. He is the one who holds together the church, his people, and the world. When we think about Jesus as the one and only, this imagery of the cornerstone is helpful. While we have Scripture to help us, pastors to guide us, and spiritual practices to develop us, only Christ is the foundation of these things. He is the cornerstone of our faith and our lives. Without him, everything would crumble.

It can be tempting to want to replace our cornerstone with something or someone other than Jesus. We rely on our partner as our foundation, or our physical health, or our wealth. But what if you lose your partner? What if your health struggles? What if you have to file for bankruptcy and lose your wealth? If these things represent your cornerstone, your life will crumble. But if *Christ* is your cornerstone, you, your life, and your faith will remain intact.

Of course, this doesn't mean that you won't have struggles in life. This doesn't mean that part of the house won't need to be rebuilt at times. But the structure as a whole will survive because Jesus—your one and only—is the one holding it all together.

READ | Psalm 118:22–24 and Ephesians 2:19–22

REFLECT

1. The psalmist prophesied the arrival of Christ in this passage. He wrote that Jesus would be "the stone the builders rejected" but that he would ultimately "become the

cornerstone" (verse 22). What are some of the ways that Jesus was rejected during his time on earth? How did he prove himself to be the cornerstone?

2. According to the apostle Paul in the Ephesians passage, how is Christ the cornerstone for the holy temple of the Lord? How is he the cornerstone for us individually?

3. What would you say is serving as the cornerstone of your life right now? Is it Jesus or something or someone else? Explain.

4. How could you better rely on Jesus as your one and only cornerstone? What would change in your life if you chose to only rely on Christ as your foundation?

PRAY | End your time in prayer. Thank Jesus for offering to be your cornerstone in this life. Ask him to help you rely on him—and only him—and center him as the foundation of your life.

-Day 2-

THE ULTIMATE AUTHORITY

We all have mixed experiences with authority figures. Some of us have had respectable authority figures in the past who were easy to follow and trust. Many of us of have had an authority figure or two whom we didn't respect or trust. We've seen some people choose to use their authority for good while others have chosen to use it for their own benefit.

Given this, thinking about Jesus as an authority over your life might be a difficult concept for you to grasp or accept. However, when we look at the Gospels, we find that the type of authority Jesus exhibited did not belittle others or hurt them. He did not exercise authority for his own gain. He did not abuse his power. He used his authority to heal, to speak up for the powerless, and to point others toward the Father.

Jesus also used his authority over the spiritual realm. He cast out demons and set people free. While we may not encounter demon possession in the same way today, as one commentator pointed out, all the demons that Jesus confronted in Scripture had three things in common: "They caused self-destructive behavior in the victim, the victim felt trapped in that condition, and they separated the victim from normal living in the family circle."[17]

You've probably encountered something like this in your life. A sin pattern, circumstance, or habit that kept you trapped, that was self-destructive, or that ostracized you from your friends and family. Know that *Jesus has power over these things*. He has *authority* over them. Take comfort in this truth. Even for someone with authority issues, that's the type of authority we could all use in our lives—one that frees us from our demons, protects us from the darkness, builds us up in the Father, and heals our brokenness.

READ | Luke 8:26–39

REFLECT

1. This story occurred right after Jesus calmed a storm on the Sea of Galilee. His power caused his disciples to ask, "Who is this? He commands even the winds and the water,

and they obey him" (Luke 8:25). When the disciples made it safely to shore, Jesus continued to display his power in this passage. What did the demon-possessed man call Jesus in verse 28? Why do you think he saw Jesus as an authority figure?

2. What did the man want from Jesus after he was set free (see verse 38)? What does this tell you about the impact that Jesus' authority had on this man?

3. What are some of the issues you are struggling with right now and need Jesus to set you free? How are these things affecting your life, faith, and relationships?

4. How does this story give you hope about Jesus' authority over these things? How would it feel—and what would it look like—to be free from these demons?

PRAY | Come before Jesus with humility. Ask him to free you from the sin, struggles, and unhealthy habits that are causing havoc in your life. Confess that you are tired of facing these struggles alone. Trust that he has the authority to get rid of them once and for all.

THE GREAT REVEALER

The rabbis of Jesus' time (and still today) were authorities on the Torah. They studied it, they preached it, and they commentated on it. If you had a question about the Scriptures, you went and asked the rabbi.

Jesus is often called a rabbi in Scripture (see, for example, Mark 9:5, Mark 11:21, and John 1:49). This is how his disciples would have viewed him: as an authority on the scriptures. They asked him hard questions. They followed him and learned from him. In one story, we read that a woman named Mary sat at Jesus' feet. In so doing, she was assuming the role of a disciple with her rabbi (see Luke 10:38–42).[18]

Today, we often take this role of Jesus for granted. We don't think of him as a teacher who could command his classroom with authority. We also don't consider how radically different he was from other rabbis of the time. "Do not resist an evil person," he said. "If anyone slaps you on the right cheek, turn to them the other cheek also" (Matthew 5:39). "You have heard that it was said, 'Love your neighbor and hate your enemy,' " he added. "But I tell you, love your enemies and pray for those who persecute you" (verses 43–44).

As we discussed in the group time, Jesus is the one and only revealer of all things. He is ready and able to teach us all these spiritual truths if we are ready and able to listen. Sadly, all too often we are *not* ready and able to listen. We are afraid of what Jesus will tell us. We are afraid of his instruction. What if he demands more of us? What if he tells us that we are falling short? But this is not the way of rabbi Jesus! When he teaches us, the lessons are of love, grace, and acceptance. They are not lessons to fear. They are lessons that will set us free from fear.

READ | Matthew 11:25–30

REFLECT

1. Jesus began this teaching with a prayer: "I praise you, Father, Lord of heaven and earth, because you have hidden these things from the wise and learned, and revealed

them to little children" (verse 25). What does Jesus go on to say about his authority and his knowledge of the Father? To whom does he reveal this knowledge?

2. In Judaism, a yoke was used as a metaphor for how the Pharisees saw God's law: as a weight they carried on their shoulders.[19] How was Jesus' yoke different from the Pharisees'? What did Jesus say we would find when we take up his yoke?

3. What questions do you have about your life? Have you brought them to Jesus? If so, what has he taught you?

4. How could you make a practice of sitting at Jesus' feet, just as Mary did, and learning from him? What would that look like for you practically?

PRAY | Put this teaching into practice in your prayer time. Bring any questions that you have about your life before Jesus. Sit at his feet and listen for him to speak to you.

THE ONE AND ONLY WAY

We don't live with much certainty in life—and certainty is not encouraged in our culture. We live in a world of many religions, many ways, and many truths. If you've been around Christianity for any amount of time, you know it can be a bit countercultural. Jesus was countercultural in his time, so this only makes sense. He claimed to be the one and only Son of God. Not one of many. Not one of a few. He claimed to be the *only* way to salvation.

Most likely, as you have progressed in your faith, you've been on a journey with this question: *Is Jesus really the one and only way to salvation?* Perhaps you believed this wholeheartedly as a new Christian . . . but now you're not so sure. Maybe you didn't believe this about Christianity at first, but now you're a fervent believer in Jesus as the only truth and way to the Father. Maybe your beliefs are unclear right now . . . somewhere in between certainty in Christ and considering other possibilities.

Questioning the ultimate authority of Christ is a quite common experience on the Christian journey. It is not a tension to ignore or a doubt to suppress. Yet sadly, that is often what we choose to do—we let the question just fester inside of us. But keeping it suppressed won't make it go away. Maybe you've heard the phrase, *"what we resist persists,"* and that is certainly true when it comes to the question of whether Jesus is *the* way or one of many ways.

So, as you read the passage below, allow yourself to sit with any tensions you feel. Don't superficially claim to believe what Jesus says. Don't feel shamed by them. Simply sit with them. See what comes up as you allow yourself to honestly explore this question.

READ | John 14:5–11

REFLECT

1. Jesus' conversation with Thomas and Philip took place on the night before his crucifixion. He had just told his disciples that he would be leaving them, saying, "If I go

90

and prepare a place for you, I will come back and take you to be with me that you also may be where I am" (John 14:3). But the disciples didn't understand what he meant. They wanted to know where Jesus was going. How does Jesus respond to them? What does he claim to be in this passage?

2. According to Jesus, how do we get to the Father? What does Jesus say that his relationship is to the Father?

3. When you read Jesus' words, "I am the way and the truth and the life" (verse 6), what thoughts and feelings does this bring up for you?

4. Assessing your belief today, do you believe Jesus is the *only* way, truth, and life? If so, how have you experienced this in Christ? If not, what are you hesitant about?

PRAY | As you end your time in prayer, be honest with Jesus about your belief in him. Tell him if you are hesitant to believe that he is the only way and ask him to reveal the truth to you.

Day 5

CATCH UP AND REFLECT

Use this time to go back and complete any study and reflection questions from previous days this week that you weren't able to finish. Make a note below of any revelations you've had and reflect on any growth or personal insights you've gained.

Spend the next two days reading chapters 9–10 of *In the Footsteps of the Savior*. Use the space below to record anything in the chapters that stands out to you or encourages you.

WEEK 5

BEFORE GROUP MEETING	Read chapters 9–10 of *In the Footsteps of the Savior* Read the Welcome section (page 97)
GROUP MEETING	Discuss the Connect questions Watch the video teaching for session 5 Discuss the questions that follow as a group Do the closing exercise and pray (pages 98–106)
PERSONAL STUDY – DAY 1	Complete the daily study (pages 108–109)
PERSONAL STUDY – DAY 2	Complete the daily study (pages 110–111)
PERSONAL STUDY – DAY 3	Complete the daily study (pages 112–113)
PERSONAL STUDY – DAY 4	Complete the daily study (pages 114–116)
PERSONAL STUDY – DAY 5 (before week 6 group meeting)	Complete the daily study (page 117) Read chapters 11–12 of *In the Footsteps of the Savior* Complete any unfinished personal studies

Garden Tomb

FOLLOWING JESUS WHEN YOU NEED HOPE

"This is the will of him who sent me, that I shall lose none of all those he has given me, but raise them up at the last day. For my Father's will is that everyone who looks to the Son and believes in him shall have eternal life, and I will raise them up at the last day."

JOHN 6:39-40

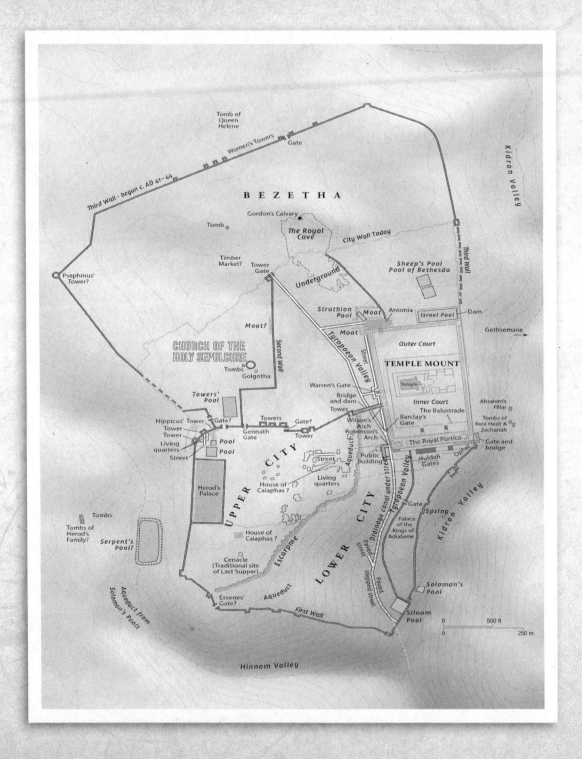

Tomb of Queen Helene

Women's Towers   Gate

Kidron Valley

Third Wall - begun c. AD 41–44

B E Z E T H A

Gordon's Calvary

The Royal Cave

City Wall Today

Tomb

Third Wall

Timber Market?   Tower Gate

Underground

Sheep's Pool Pool of Bethesda

Psephinus' Tower?

Struthion Pool   *Moat*

Antonia   *Israel Pool*   Dam

Moat?

Moat

Tyropoeon Valley

Gethsemane

CHURCH OF THE HOLY SEPULCHRE

Tombs   Golgotha

Second Wall

Street

Outer Court

TEMPLE MOUNT

Temple

Warren's Gate

Towers' Pool

Inner Court

The Balustrade

Absalom's Pillar

Tombs of Beni Hezir & Zechariah

Hippicus' Tower   Gate?

Tower   Tower

Living quarters

Street

Towers   Gate?

Gennath Gate   Tower

Bridge and dam Tower

Wilson's Arch   Barclay's Gate

Robinson's Arch

The Royal Portico

Gate and bridge

Pool   Pool

U P P E R   C I T Y

Street

Street

Public Building

Huldah Gates

Ophel

Herod's Palace

House of Caiaphas

Living quarters

Aqueduct

Kidron Valley

Gate

Spring

Palace of the Kings of Adiabene

Tyropoeon Valley

Tombs

Tombs of Herod's Family?

Serpent's Pool?

House of Caiaphas

L O W E R   C I T Y

Drainage canal under street

Paved stepped street

Solomon's Pool

Kidron Valley

Cenacle (Traditional site of Last Supper)

Escarpme

Paved street

Essenes' Gate?   Aqueduct   First Wall

Siloam Pool

0   500 ft.

0   250 m.

Aqueduct from Solomon's Pools

Hinnom Valley

Welcome | READ ON YOUR OWN

All four Gospels report that a man named Joseph of Arimathea assumed responsibility for Jesus' burial after his crucifixion. Joseph was a member of the Jewish ruling council but also a supporter of Christ. When he learned of Jesus' death, he went to Pilate, the Roman governor, and received permission to take the body of Jesus and place it in a tomb.

Little else is known about Joseph. Even the location of his hometown, Arimathea, is uncertain. It is also not known exactly where Jesus was buried. Some believe it was in what today is called the Garden Tomb, located just outside the old city walls of Jerusalem. The tomb's small entrance is carved into the side of a rock that leads into a low-ceilinged cave. On one of the walls of the cave is a faded cross, painted during the Crusader era, which indicates Christians have been observing this site as Jesus' tomb for hundreds of years.

Wherever Jesus' tomb is actually located, the most important thing to know about it is this: *it's empty*. Jesus rose from the dead. If you are a Christian, you know this and believe it to be true. But how often do you consider what Jesus' resurrection means for you, your soul, and your body after you die? What exactly happens when this life ends?

Perhaps this question has plagued you. Perhaps you've avoided it. Perhaps you've debated it with fervor. Regardless, in this session, you will look at what the Bible has to say about it. When you study God's Word, you *can* get a sense of where you're going after you die and how you will get there. All you have to do is pay attention to what it says.

Connect | 15 MINUTES

Get the session started by choosing one of the following questions to discuss as a group:

- What is a key insight or takeaway from last week's personal study that you would like to share with the group?

— *or* —

- What were you taught about heaven or the afterlife when you were younger?

Watch | 20 MINUTES

Now watch the video for this session. As you watch, use the following outline to record any thoughts or concepts that stand out to you.

I. The physical resurrection of Jesus Christ

    A. Sunday morning after the crucifixion. We don't know what the Roman executioner was wondering about, but know it wasn't about that fellow he had nailed to a cross and pierced with a spear. Jesus was dead and buried. Yesterday's news . . . right?

    B. Jesus marched out of the tomb, not spiritually raised, but physically raised. The women and disciples did not see a phantom or experience a sentiment. They saw Jesus in the flesh.

    C. They saw him eat. They touched him. They insisted. Paul says, "After that He was seen by over five hundred brethren at once" (1 Corinthians 15:6 NKJV).

II. What the resurrection means for us

    A. What happens to believers? Because the tomb is empty, the promise of Christ is not. And the promise of Christ? "Death has been swallowed up in victory" (1 Corinthians 15:54).

        1. If you trust Christ with your life, he will take care of your death. Your spirit will immediately enter into the presence of God. You will enjoy conscious fellowship with your heavenly Father and all those who have gone before. Your body will join you later.

        2. We believe this to be true because of what Paul wrote: "We are confident, I say, and would prefer to be away from the body and at home with the Lord" (2 Corinthians 5:8).

        3. Jesus said to the thief on the cross, "Today you will be with me in paradise" (Luke 23:43). *Today.* The thief closed his eyes on earth and he awoke in paradise.

B. Paradise is the first stage of heaven but not the final version of heaven. At a certain point, known today only by God, our bodies will be called out of the grave.

C. Jesus' resurrection is not only proof of your own resurrection but also a picture of it. Just as Jesus rose from the dead in a physical, touchable, imperishable body, so you will step forth in a physical, touchable, and *imperishable* body. This is the promise of Christ.

III. What the resurrection means for our world

A. Envision this world as it was intended to be. Isaiah wrote that in that day, "The wolf will live with the lamb, the leopard will lie down with the goat, the calf and the lion and the yearling together; and a little child will lead them" (Isaiah 11:6). Nature and humanity at peace.

B. No one, and no thing, will rebel against God. All of us, nature and humanity, will defer to the risen King. "No longer will there be any curse" (Revelation 22:3).

C. There will be no more curse because there will be no more devil. He will be cast into the pit that was "prepared for the devil and his angels" (Matthew 25:41).

IV. The question the resurrection compels us to answer

A. So here's the question: *Have you made the Easter miracle your hope for your life?*

B. Philip Yancey said, "The reason I believe in Jesus is because of Jesus . . . and because Plan B stinks." With all due respect to different thoughts and philosophies—Plan B is terrible.

C. Plan A is a resurrected body, on a resurrected planet, in the presence of a resurrected Lord, ever living in peace in a kingdom. God will have his Garden of Eden.

D. We do not want to be a part of a system that says if we're good enough, God will save us. Because we're not good enough. But we will take the one that says Jesus *was* good enough for us and he *will* save us.

GARDEN TOMB

JERUSALEM

While we don't know for certain the location of the tomb that Jesus borrowed before he rose from the dead, we do know something about first-century Jewish burial practices. Typical Jewish tombs had two chambers. The outer chamber was used to prepare the body for burial, while the inner chamber was used for the burial itself. As part of the preparation process, the body would be treated in the outer chamber with spices and perfumes. Mourning ceremonies would take place, and then the body would be laid on a ledge in the inner chamber. The tomb would be sealed with a large disc-shaped stone that rolled in a trench in front of it.

The tomb would remain sealed until the family returned to bury another member or collect the bones of the deceased. These bones would be placed in a small box called an ossuary. Sometimes, these boxes would be adorned with decorative designs, and in many cases the family name would be inscribed on the side. The ossuary would be placed in a small niche cut into the rock on one side of the inner chamber. As the years passed, the bones from several people in the same family would be collected and also placed in the box.

In Jesus' case, the Gospels reveal that his tomb was sealed before his body was prepared (see Matthew 27:57–66) and that he arose from the dead before his friends could return to complete the burial (see 28:1–6). Jesus was also placed in a tomb owned not by a family member but by Joseph of Arimathea (see 27:59–60). Joseph was evidently very wealthy, as only a rich person would have been able to afford a tomb with a stone large enough to cause the women who visited on Sunday to be concerned they could not move it (see Mark 16:1–3).[20]

SIGNIFICANT EVENTS IN AND AROUND JESUS' TOMB[21]

The women arrive at the tomb find the stone rolled away	Luke 24:2–9
Mary Magdalene and the other Mary see the angel	Matthew 28:1–8
Peter and John arrive at the tomb, look in, and depart	John 20:3–10
Mary Magdalene sees two angels and then Jesus	John 20:11–18
The risen Christ sends her to inform the disciples	John 20:17–18
The women are met by the risen Christ	Matthew 28:9–10

Discuss | 35 MINUTES

Take some time to discuss what you just watched by answering the following questions. Use the suggested questions to begin your discussion, and then choose any of the additional questions as time allows.

Suggested Questions

1. What is your current belief or understanding about what happens to us after we die? Where does this belief come from?

2. Ask someone to read aloud Matthew 28:1–10. How did Mary and Mary Magdalene respond to seeing Jesus? What does their response tell you about what kind of resurrection this was (physical or spiritual)? Why does this matter?

3. Ask someone to read aloud Luke 23:39-43. What does this story tell you about what happens the moment you die? Do you find this hopeful? Why or why not?

4. Now have someone read aloud 2 Corinthians 5:6–10. What does it mean to be "away" from our bodies? What is Paul saying about our resurrection in this passage?

Additional Questions

5. What are you most looking forward to in the resurrection as it relates to your physical body? How does this week's teaching give you hope about what is to come?

6. Paul wrote that Christ will one day "transform our lowly bodies so that they will be like his glorious body" (Philippians 3:21). What does mean when he refers to Christ's "glorious body"? What would your body be like if it were glorious?

7. Ask someone to read aloud Isaiah 11:6–9. What imagery sticks out to you in this passage? What would your neighborhood, community, or city look like if it were made into the type of place that Isaiah described in these verses?

8. Have you made the Easter miracle your hope for your life? If so, what hope has this provided for you? If not, what is holding you back?

Respond | 10 MINUTES

Review the outline for the video teaching and any notes you took. In the space below, write down your most significant takeaway from this session.

Pray | 10 MINUTES

End your time by praying together as a group, asking the Lord to fill all the members with hope as you consider Jesus' resurrection and the promise that it holds for our own physical resurrection. Ask if anyone has any prayer requests to share. Write those requests down in the space below so you and your group members can pray about them in the week ahead.

Name   Request

Personal Study

As you discussed in your group time this week, Jesus' resurrection points to what will happen to us, his followers, after we die. We will be given resurrected bodies to enjoy in a redeemed world. As you explore this theme in this week's personal study, write down your responses to the questions in the spaces provided, as you will be given a few minutes to share your insights at the start of the next session if you are doing this study with others. If you are reading *In the Footsteps of the Savior* alongside this study, first review chapters 9–10 in the book.

RESURRECTION POWER

Jesus' resurrection proved his power over death and foreshadowed the resurrection that all believers will one day experience when they are reunited with their bodies in the presence of God. But Christ's resurrection also revealed his power to bring *anything* dead to life. For it is not just our bodies that experience death and need resurrection power.

When we come to know Christ, we experience a type of resurrection from our old lives to our new. This is the symbolism of baptism. When you go under the water, the pastor says something along the lines of, "You have died to your sins." Then, when you are raised out of the water, the pastor declares, "You are raised to new life!"

In Christ, resurrection power is within you. Oswald Chambers called this "co-resurrection." As he explained, "I can have the resurrection life of Jesus here and now, and it will exhibit itself through holiness. The idea all through the apostle Paul's writings is that after the decision to be identified with Jesus in His death has been made, the resurrection life of Jesus penetrates every bit of my human nature."[22]

In Christ, we are resurrected as new creations here and now. This transformation doesn't start with heaven. It starts with Jesus. This means this transformation from death to life can happen in all areas of our lives—our work, our relationships, our health, our hearts. Jesus' resurrection power isn't reserved for the grave or the tomb. It's living and breathing within us right now by the power of the Holy Spirit, who is ready to change and transform any and everything we thought was dead and beyond life.

For in Christ, nothing is!

READ | Romans 8:9–11

REFLECT

1. This is likely one of the passages that Oswald Chambers had in mind when he said that one of Paul's major themes in his writings was that after our conversion, "the

resurrection life of Jesus" penetrates every part of our nature. According to Paul in this passage, what happens to our bodies if Christ is in us?

2. Paul wrote that believers in Christ are "not in the realm of the flesh but are in the realm of the Spirit." What does it mean to live in the realm of the Spirit?

3. How have you experienced resurrection power in your life?

4. Where do you need resurrection power in your life today? Why?

PRAY | Spend some time in prayer remembering or noticing examples of resurrection in your life, in the life of others, or in nature. Write these examples down. Give thanks to God for them and ask Jesus to give you resurrection where you need it most today.

A WHOLE BODY

As you saw in this week's teaching, when the thief on the cross asked Jesus to remember him, the Lord promised that he would be with him that day in paradise (see Luke 23:43). The thief closed his eyes on earth and awoke in paradise. But paradise is not the final version of heaven. At a certain point, our bodies will someday be called out of the grave and resurrected.

God loves our bodies. After all, it was his idea to create them. Unfortunately, in our culture today, we are not always taught to have that same love or acceptance for our bodies. From a young age, we receive messages about what our body should look like and how it should perform. We idealize young, thin, strong, and able bodies. But what if our bodies don't look that way? What if we're not young? What if we're not thin? What if we're not strong? What if we have a disability? What if we're suffering from an ongoing illness?

The Bible reveals that when we die, our bodies will finally be whole. But what do we do in the meantime? Should we reject our bodies in hopes of the one that is to come? Or is it possible to live at peace with our earthly bodies *and* live in hope for the day our bodies are made whole? Jesus gives us a hint. The way he treated those who lived in sick, unwell, or marginalized bodies tells us how we can treat and accept our own bodies. He didn't reject the sick. He spent time with them and even healed them. He didn't ignore or disrespect women for being in a female body, which was common for the time. He spoke to them and even equipped them for ministry, even women who were part of a "taboo" race (see John 4:4–42).

Although we live in a culture that likes to dictate what bodies are "good" and what bodies are "bad," including our own, Jesus did not judge others in this way. He accepted all bodies, no matter their gender, ailment, or appearance. Could you do the same with yours?

READ | John 9:1–11

REFLECT

1. Jewish teachers believed suffering was a consequence of sin, which is likely why the disciples asked Jesus what the blind man had done to deserve his blindness.[23] But

Jesus had a different response. What did he say was the reason this man was blind? What does this tell you about how Jesus viewed this man's suffering?

2. What did Jesus do to heal the man? How do you think those who witnessed this miracle would have felt about Jesus' interactions with the blind man?

3. How do you feel about your body? Do you feel critical of it or accepting of it? Perhaps it depends on the day? Explain your answer.

4. Considering this story, how do you think Jesus feels about your body? What would it look like to accept your body the way that God accepts it?

PRAY | Before you pray today, practice being present in your body. Sit in a comfortable position, close your eyes, and notice where your body is making contact with the chair, couch, or floor. Put your hand on your chest and feel breath move up and down. Once you've settled into feeling present in your body, ask God to help you accept your body as it is right now.

-Day 3-

FEAR OF DEATH

Maybe death feels a long way off to you. You rarely think about it. Maybe it feels close and becomes more of a reality every day. Maybe you know someone who succumbed to death too soon and you fear the same will happen to you. Regardless of where you are today, your relationship with death will change over time. Just because you're a Christian doesn't mean that you won't have questions and concerns about it. Even if you are confident in Christ, it doesn't mean that you won't be fearful at times of the prospect of death.

Fortunately, the Bible doesn't shy from the topic of death like we so often do. Jesus frequently talked about his own death when he was with his disciples—even though they didn't understand what he meant until they witnessed the crucifixion (see John 13:33; 14:1–4). Jesus talked about where he was going after he died. He didn't avoid the subject. He also grieved for those who had died, such as he did for his friend Lazarus (see 11:35).

Jesus was familiar with death. He witnessed it and experienced it himself. He talked about it freely and understood the fear of it. Remember his anxiety in the Garden of Gethsemane on the night before his crucifixion (see Luke 22:42)? The topic we like to avoid the most . . . Jesus confronted head on. Maybe he was trying to tell us something. Maybe he was setting an example of how to live with the knowledge of death, our own and those we love.

We often fear what we don't understand, so fearing death is understandable. It's a mystery. We don't get a trial run at death (well, at least most of us don't). But death is not a mystery to Christ. In him, we know we have a Savior who understands death, our fear of it, and exactly what happens to us when it happens.

He has been there. He lived to tell us about it.

READ | 1 Corinthians 15:51–58

REFLECT

1. Paul's work was dangerous. He was spreading the gospel in places where people didn't always want to hear it. As a result, as he states in this passage, he was no stranger to

being beaten and put in prison. He knew very well what it was like to be near death and what it was like to risk his life. Yet he had so much hope in the face of death because he believed in the resurrection! According to this passage, what three things did Jesus' resurrection abolish? How are those three things connected?

2. What did Paul instruct us to do now that death has been swallowed by life?

3. Take a moment to consider your "relationship" with death. Maybe it feels a long way off, or maybe it feels close. What are your thoughts and feelings about death?

4. How does this passage from the apostle Paul give you hope for the mystery and wonder of death and its aftermath?

PRAY | Come before your heavenly Father today and present any fears or concerns that you have about death. Ask him to help you understand that death has been swallowed up in victory and what that really means in your life. Ask him to help you believe in this promise.

— Day 4 —

PEACE ON EARTH

What do you think about when you consider heaven? What do you hope will be there? *Who* do you hope will be there? What do you hope you will be able to do, see, hear, even taste?

When we think about heaven, we tend to think about what makes us happy. And although heaven will undoubtedly be a joyful place, the major theme in Scripture used to describe God's eternal kingdom is not happiness but *peace*. This peace we read about echoes the peace that Adam and Eve enjoyed with God in the Garden of Eden. In many ways, heaven is a restoration of Eden, and Jesus is the one responsible for that restoration. Jesus is the "Prince of Peace" and "of the greatness of his government and peace there will be no end" (Isaiah 9:6–7).

Now, though we are promised peace for eternity, we aren't promised that peace is only *for* eternity. We are called to be peacemakers in our earthly lives. Jesus said, "Blessed are the peacemakers, for they will be called children of God" (Matthew 5:9). Notice that Jesus said peace*makers*, not peace*keepers*. Peace takes work! If you've ever been in conflict with a loved one, you know that peace doesn't just happen. You have to talk through the conflict, find a compromise, and be honest about your feelings so you can find peace.

The work of the Christ follower is to bring God's kingdom to this earth. We aren't supposed to wait until we get to heaven. That is where God's work will be completed, but as you read in yesterday's passage, "Throw yourselves into the work of the Master, confident that nothing you do for him is a waste of time or effort" (1 Corinthians 15:58 MSG). While we wait on heaven, we can work to bring heaven to earth by working toward peace in our relationships, our homes, and our communities—a peace that echoes Eden.

READ | Genesis 2:8–10 and Revelation 22:1–5

REFLECT

1. The opening chapters of Genesis reveal that God created a harmonious garden for Adam and Eve, the first humans, to live in and enjoy. But that harmony would be

disrupted when they ate from the tree of the knowledge of good and evil—a sin that led to them being banished and cursed (see Genesis 3). What was the Garden of Eden like? How did it represent harmony among God, humans, and nature?

2. The apostle John witnessed a restoration of Eden in his vision. What does the tree of life represent in Revelation 22:2? How has peace been restored?

3. Where do you need peace in your life? Or where do you see a need for peace in your community? How does this lack of peace affect you or your community?

4. How might God be calling you to be a peacemaker, whether that's in your own relationships, your work, or within your community?

PRAY | Ask God how you can bring his kingdom to earth by doing the hard work of peacemaking. Also ask him to help you reconcile and restore any relationships that are broken. Whatever you are hesitant about today, bring those concerns to the Prince of Peace.

Day 5

CATCH UP AND REFLECT

Use this time to go back and complete any study and reflection questions from previous days this week that you weren't able to finish. Make a note below of any revelations you've had and reflect on any growth or personal insights you've gained.

Spend the next two days reading chapters 11–12 of *In the Footsteps of the Savior*. Use the space below to record anything in the chapters that stands out to you or encourages you.

WEEK 6

BEFORE GROUP MEETING	Read chapters 11–12 of *In the Footsteps of the Savior* Read the Welcome section (page 121)
GROUP MEETING	Discuss the Connect questions Watch the video teaching for session 6 Discuss the questions that follow as a group Do the closing exercise and pray (pages 122–130)
PERSONAL STUDY – DAY 1	Complete the daily study (pages 132–133)
PERSONAL STUDY – DAY 2	Complete the daily study (pages 134–135)
PERSONAL STUDY – DAY 3	Complete the daily study (pages 136–137)
PERSONAL STUDY – DAY 4	Complete the daily study (pages 138–140)
PERSONAL STUDY – DAY 5 (personal wrap-up of the study)	Complete the daily study (page 141) Connect with your group about the next study that you want to go through together

Caesarea by the Sea

FOLLOWING JESUS WHEN YOU NEED GRACE

It is by grace you have been saved, through faith—and this is not from yourselves, it is the gift of God—not by works, so that no one can boast. For we are God's handiwork, created in Christ Jesus to do good works, which God prepared in advance for us to do.

EPHESIANS 2:8-10

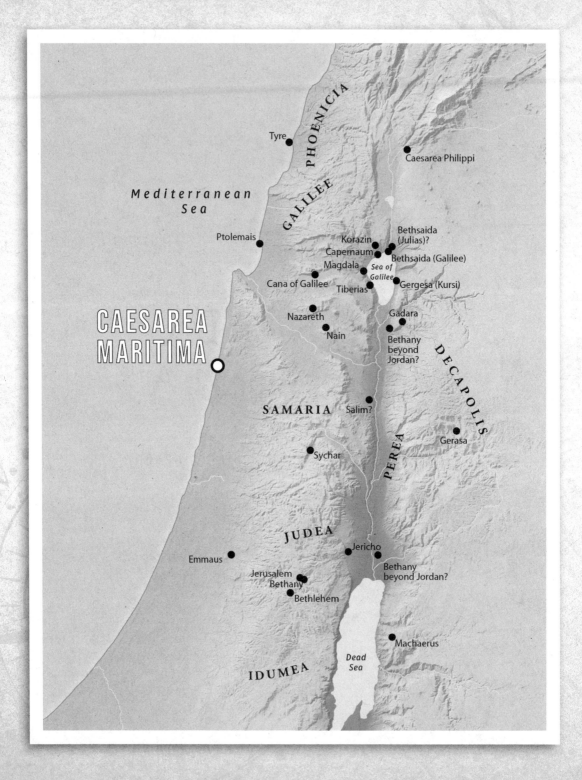

Tyre

PHOENICIA

Caesarea Philippi

Mediterranean Sea

GALILEE

Ptolemais

Korazin

Bethsaida (Julias)?

Capernaum

Bethsaida (Galilee)

Magdala

Sea of Galilee

Cana of Galilee

Tiberias

Gergesa (Kursi)

Nazareth

Gadara

Nain

Bethany beyond Jordan?

CAESAREA MARITIMA

DECAPOLIS

SAMARIA

Salim?

PEREA

Sychar

Gerasa

JUDEA

Emmaus

Jericho

Bethany beyond Jordan?

Jerusalem
Bethany

Bethlehem

Machaerus

Dead Sea

IDUMEA

Welcome | READ ON YOUR OWN

Caesarea by the Sea is one of the more breathtaking ruins in Israel. Located right on the Mediterranean Sea, one can still see the layout of Herod the Great's palace, which was built in 22 BC when he was the king of Judea. A longtime Roman stronghold, Caesarea was different from the city of Jerusalem just a few miles away. It was more Gentile than Jew and more Roman than Hebrew.

The book of Acts relates that a Roman army officer named Cornelius lived in Caesarea. A few miles south of the city was Joppa, the town where the disciple Peter was staying. Peter and Cornelius could not have been more different, but they would be called by the same God to change the way Jews and new Christians saw the Gentiles . . . and vice versa.

A great divide had existed in the early church between believers who came from a Jewish background and those who came from a Gentile background. But as you will see in this session, a miracle was about to happen that would forever break down the walls between who was considered "in" and "out" of God's kingdom. These events would forever prove that Jesus' message was for *everyone*. His love was for *everyone*. His sacrifice for *everyone*.

The spirit of Peter and Cornelius' mission is alive and well today. How many of us have had to change our minds about someone or an entire people group? How many of us have experienced prejudice or felt prejudice toward others? It's a common symptom of the human condition—to judge and ostracize rather than welcome. This is the *good news*. No one is beyond Jesus. No one is beyond forgiveness. No one is beyond acceptance into God's family.

Connect | 15 MINUTES

Get the session started by choosing one of the following questions to discuss as a group:

- What is a key insight or takeaway from last week's personal study that you would like to share with the group?

— *or* —

- Think of some times in your life that you were excluded because you were not considered part of the group. How did that make you feel?

Watch | 20 MINUTES

Now watch the video for this session. As you watch, use the following outline to record any thoughts or concepts that stand out to you.

I. Why people like clubs—knowing who is *in* and who is *out*

A. Clubs have a way of tidying up the world. They create insiders and outsiders. Since we tend to cluster according to what we have in common, clubs eliminate surprises. The people in the club tend to look alike, believe alike, and think alike.

B. Maybe this is why Jesus did not start a club. He was more keen on welcoming people in than in keeping people out. Remember how he was introduced to the world in John's Gospel: "The Word became flesh . . . and moved into the neighborhood" (John 1:14 MSG).

C. Jesus didn't start a clubhouse but created a *lighthouse*. He could hardly demonstrate this lighthouse view more clearly than he did right in the story of Peter and Cornelius.

II. God sends a vision to Peter to reveal who is *in* and who is *out* of his kingdom

    A. An impassable yawn stretched between Jews and Gentiles in the days of the early church. No Jew would have anything to do with a Gentile. Unless, of course, that Jew was named Jesus.

    B. Scripture said to keep his distance from the Gentiles. But his Christ said to build a bridge. Peter had to make a choice, which came in the form of a Gentile named Cornelius.

        1. Cornelius was an officer in the Roman army. He ate the wrong food, hung out with the wrong crowd, and he swore allegiance to Caesar. But he also helped needy people, sympathized with Jewish ethics, and was on a first-name basis with an angel.

        2. Peter fell into a trance and saw an object like a great sheet bound at the four corners descend to earth. In it were all kinds of four-footed animals, wild beasts, creeping things, and birds of the air. A voice said to him, "Rise, Peter; kill and eat" (Acts 10:13 NKJV).

3. Peter resolutely refused. "Not so, Lord! For I have never eaten anything common or unclean" (Acts 10:14 NKJV). But God wasn't kidding. He three-repeated the vision.

C. Peter was left in a quandary with the question of the kingdom: *If it's okay to eat Gentile food, is it okay to be friends with the Gentiles?*

III. Peter's conclusion on who should be *in* and who should be *out* of the church

A. The Holy Spirit told Peter, "Behold, three men are seeking you. Arise therefore, go down and go with them, doubting nothing; for I have sent them" (Acts 10:19–20 NKJV). God was correcting Peter's people vision. Those men at the door were not Gentiles but God's creation.

B. Peter went against the current of his culture and he invited the messengers to spend the night with him. Big step. Then he headed out the next morning to meet Cornelius.

C. Peter told Cornelius about Jesus, and before he could even issue an altar call, the Holy Spirit fell. Soon Cornelius and the members of his household were replicating the Pentecost miracle.

D. What do we do with this story? Underline verse 28: "God has shown me that I should not call any man common or unclean" (Acts 10:28 NKJV). A breakthrough in the history of the church.

IV. Ten years later . . . the church still debates who is *in* and who is *out*

A. Some ten years later, in the city of Jerusalem, the Jews were resisting the Gentiles again. "Certain people came down from Judea to Antioch and were teaching the believers: 'Unless you are circumcised, according to the custom taught by Moses, you cannot be saved'" (Acts 15:1).

B. These "certain men" were Pharisees. When unkosher Gentiles began showing up at their church, they had to add a few requirements. Good-news *grace* quickly became bad-news *requirements*.

C. So a conference was called. "The apostles and elders came together to consider this matter" Acts 15:6 NKJV). On the table was the question, *Is God's grace sufficient for salvation*?

   1. Grace-a-lots: The Pharisees believed God's grace accomplished a lot. In the rowboat of salvation, God takes one oar and we take the other. God does his part. We do our part.

   2. Grace alone: Peter reminded the council of the conversion of Cornelius. What saved the Jews would save the Gentiles. Not through the work of a devoted saint, the penance of the church, nor through tithes or prayers, but only through the grace of Christ.

D. It was time for Peter to step off the stage and pass the baton to Paul. His final words in Scripture: "But we believe that through the grace of the Lord Jesus Christ we shall be saved in the same manner as they" (Acts 15:11 NKJV).

CAESAREA BY THE SEA

CAESAREA MARITIMA

In 30 BC, the site that would become Caesarea Maritima, along with all of Judea, was given to King Herod the Great by the Roman emperor Caesar Augustus. At that time the location was called Straton's Tower, so named after an ancient king of Sidon, and had already been in existence for centuries as a trading village. But under the governance of King Herod, the city would undergo vast changes and be transformed into a major port city in the region.

In addition to other construction projects in the city, Herod built a palace, aqueducts (to bring water from springs in the northeast), an arena, a marketplace, bathhouses, a temple dedicated to Caesar and Rome, and other imposing buildings. Yet the real masterpiece of the city was its deep-sea harbor named Sabastos, which at its height was one of the most impressive harbors in the world. The historian Josephus would later write, "Although the location was generally unfavorable, [Herod] contended with the difficulties so well that the solidity of the construction could not be overcome by the sea."

Under Herod's rule, the city grew to more than 125,000 people, in time becoming the largest city in Judea. After Herod's death in AD 6, Judea became a Roman province, and Caesarea Maritima replaced Jerusalem as its civilian and military capital. The city also became the official residence of Judea's governors, including the Roman prefect Pontius Pilate and the Roman procurator Antonius Felix, each of whom are named in the New Testament.[24]

SIGNIFICANT EVENTS THAT TOOK PLACE NEAR CAESAREA	
Cornelius has a vison and sends men to Joppa to find Peter	Acts 10:1–48
Paul lands in Caesarea after his second missionary journey	Acts 18:22
Paul visits Philip the Evangelist after his third missionary journey	Acts 21:8–9
Agabus prophesizes that Paul will be handed over to the Romans	Acts 21:10–11
Paul is arrested and taken to Governor Felix	Acts 23:23–24
Paul is imprisoned in Caesarea for two years	Acts 24:27
Paul appears before Governor Festus	Acts 25:6–7
Paul appears before King Agrippa and Bernice	Acts 25:23
Paul boards a ship headed for Rome	Acts 27:1–2

Discuss | 35 MINUTES

Take some time to discuss what you just watched by answering the following questions. Use the suggested questions to begin your discussion, and then choose any of the additional questions as time allows.

Suggested Questions

1. Take a few minutes on your own to read the full story of Peter and Cornelius told in Acts 10. Who was Cornelius? Why do you think he was visited by the angel?

2. Why do you think God chose food to explain to Peter what is clean and unclean? (See Leviticus 11 to read about the dietary laws given to Moses and the Israelites.)

3. What did Peter's sermon declare to the Jews and Gentiles who were gathered together?

4. What did you once consider "unclean" or taboo or un-Christian that you no longer do? How did God change your mind about this?

Additional Questions

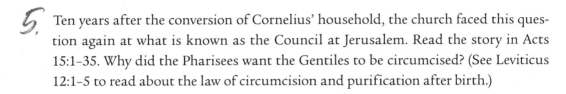 Ten years after the conversion of Cornelius' household, the church faced this question again at what is known as the Council at Jerusalem. Read the story in Acts 15:1–35. Why did the Pharisees want the Gentiles to be circumcised? (See Leviticus 12:1–5 to read about the law of circumcision and purification after birth.)

6. What did Peter say in his address to the council members? What did Paul and Barnabas say? What ruling did James ultimately make to resolve the matter?

7. What is the difference between "grace-a-lot" and "grace alone"? Which doctrine were you taught? Where do you fall today on the spectrum of grace-a-lot versus grace alone?

8. Where are you tempted to have a grace-a-lot mindset when it comes to others? How could you let go of the grace-a-lot mindset in this area of your life?

Respond | 10 MINUTES

Review the outline for the video teaching and any notes you took. In the space below, write down your most significant takeaway from this session.

Pray | 10 MINUTES

End your time by praying as a group, thanking God that he does not exclude anyone from his grace. Ask if anyone has any prayer requests to share. Write those requests down in the space below so you and your group members can pray about them in the week ahead.

Name   Request

Personal Study

As you discussed in your group time this week, Jesus came into this world to bring the message of salvation to *everyone* who believes. He broke down the cultural barriers that existed in his day of exactly who should be considered "in" and "out" of God's kingdom—and we are the beneficiaries as a result. As you explore this theme in this week's final personal study, write down your responses to the questions in the spaces provided. If you are reading *In the Footsteps of the Savior* alongside this study, first review chapters 11–12 in the book.

-Day 1-

OLD WAY VS. NEW WAY

You may have read parts of Leviticus during your group session this week. Leviticus is a book full of instructions given to Moses by God for the Hebrew people. The Israelites were prone to straying from God's will. The Lord wanted to live among his people, but their sin prevented him from doing it. So God created laws so that his people would remain clean through certain practices and rituals and so that he could continue living among them.[25]

Eating certain foods, not touching anything related to death, and performing sacrifices helped the Israelites maintain their purity and standing before God. These laws set the Israelites apart from their Canaanite (or "Gentile") neighbors. Therefore, to the Israelites, the Gentiles were typically viewed as unclean and not worthy of being in God's presence.

Understanding this helps us to understand why it was so significant for Peter to say that the Gentiles' hearts had been purified by faith (see Acts 15:9). For hundreds of years, the Jews had attained purity one way—by keeping the law. Now Peter was saying *anyone* could be made pure. They did not have to keep the law. Such a declaration would have been shocking to the Jewish people of the day. You can see why many would be reluctant to believe it.

After all, Peter was asking them to do nothing less than *completely change the way they thought about purity and what it takes to be in God's presence.* Jesus had disrupted the entire system of purity through his sacrifice on the cross. He made it possible for anyone's heart to be made clean and for anyone to enter God's presence. It was "disruptive theology" back then. But it can still be disruptive to our theologies and ways of understanding today.

READ | Acts 28:23–32

REFLECT

1. In this passage, Paul is speaking to Jewish officials while he is under house arrest in Rome. Luke describes his situation in the book of Acts: "When we got to Rome, Paul was allowed to live by himself, with a soldier to guard him. Three days later he called together the local Jewish leaders" (28:16–17). In Paul's meeting with the Jewish leaders, he quotes Isaiah 6:9–10, with which this audience would have been very familiar. According to Acts 28:25, how did these Jewish officials respond to him?

2. Why do you think the Jewish officials were so offended by Paul's words?

3. What are some of the ways the gospel offends people today? Why do you think it is so difficult for some people to accept the good news that Christ offers?

4. Who are the "Gentiles" in your life—the people you tend to avoid, or dislike, or don't understand? How does it feel to know that even these people are purified in the name of Jesus?

PRAY | Think more about the "Gentiles" in your life who you tend to avoid, dislike, and not understand. Confess to Jesus the people you distance yourself from or are tempted to believe are beyond salvation. Ask him to help you see these people in a brand-new way.

CLUBHOUSE VS. LIGHTHOUSE

Belonging is crucial to living. It's why our ancestors formed tribes. Food, water, and safety were only guaranteed in a group, and people couldn't survive alone. Although our physical needs are met differently today, we've held onto this tribal mindset. It's evolved into social clubs, fitting into a certain economic status, having a social media platform, having a certain degree. We have all kinds of measures to dictate who is in and who is out.

We all know what it's like to feel rejected from those social constructs. Rejection makes us feel as if we are not enough—not attractive enough, smart enough, rich enough, *something* enough. Perhaps knowing the sting of rejection makes getting into the "club" feel that much better. The exclusive group, job, or friend selects you, and you jump in without considering those who are left behind. Finally, you belong somewhere, and you cling to it like your life depends on it. Because, in a way, like it did for our ancestors, it does.

This is why Jesus' approach to the clubhouse is so radical. He dismantled it and exposed it for what it was: a way to reject others in order to feel better about ourselves. Jesus doesn't want us to build clubhouses. He wants us to be a lighthouse. Clubhouses have secret doors and entryways. Lighthouses shine bright for all to see. Clubhouses allow you to enter if you're polished, cleaned up, and put together. Lighthouses are there for those who are in distress, tossed by the waves, and need a safe place to anchor.

Clubhouses reject and select. Lighthouses draw in and welcome anyone who sees them. They point people to the ultimate light and ultimate source of belonging: Jesus Christ.

READ | Matthew 5:14–16

REFLECT

1. Jesus preached these words in the Sermon on the Mount. In the verses before, he listed the type of people who are blessed: "Blessed are the poor in spirit . . . blessed are the peacemakers . . . blessed are those who are persecuted" (verses 3, 9, 10). Knowing this, what type of person does Jesus say is the light of the world? How does this differ from the type of people we tend to elevate today?

2. According to verse 16, what is the ultimate goal for showing our light?

3. How has someone been a lighthouse for you—shown you the way to Jesus and made you feel like you belong?

4. How could you be a lighthouse for those around you?

PRAY | In your prayer time today, thank God for the lights in your life that have shown you the way. Ask him how you could be a light to others.

—Day 3—

GRACE ALONE VS. GRACE-A-LOT

This week, you read about the Council at Jerusalem (see Acts 15). This council was called because certain Jewish believers were stating that Gentile believers needed to be circumcised (and follow other Jewish religious practices) in order to be considered part of the church. The thinking was that Gentiles who converted to Judaism did so through circumcision and baptism—so why wouldn't it be the same for Gentiles converting to Christianity?[26]

At the time, Christianity was considered a *sect* of Judaism, since it was started by a Jew (Jesus) and first followed by Jews (the disciples and early believers). It was not the world religion that it is today. So you can't blame these Jewish believers for their mindset and requirements. They were simply following the law as they understood it. (And during this time, a stricter school of Pharisees known as the Shammai were in power, so it could be this type of strict, law-abiding leadership was trickling down and affecting early Christians.[27])

The church was employing a grace-a-lot mindset. They were saying that grace will get you *most* of the way there, but you must be circumcised or baptized or _____ (fill in the blank) to get the rest of the way there. Such a mindset is still alive today—in our churches and in our own hearts. The free nature of grace is still hard for us to believe!

The grace alone mindset was as counter to Jewish thinking back in Jesus' day and it is counter to our thinking today. Even when you've accepted him as your Savior, it is tempting to want to pick up the other oar and start paddling to get yourself the rest of the way. But grace alone tells you to put the oar down. Let grace alone do the work and take you home.

READ | Ephesians 2:1–9

REFLECT

1. Considering the context you've just read, it's understandable that Paul would need to preach the message of the gospel plainly and directly to new Christian believers.

This is what he was doing in this passage that he wrote to the church in Ephesus. According to Paul's words in verse 4, why did God make us alive with Christ?

2. Paul lays out our condition before we encounter Christ—we are "dead in [our] transgressions and sins" (verse 1), "disobedient" (verse 2), and "deserving of [God's] wrath" (verse 3). But instead of condemning us to eternal judgment, God gives us new life in Christ. According to verses 8–9, how do we get this grace from God?

3. When it comes to the gospel and grace, what is difficult for you to believe? Why?

4. If you were to put down your "oar" today and fully embrace the grace alone mindset, what would change? How would *you* change? How would your life look different?

PRAY | For your prayer time today, meditate on Ephesians 2:4–9. Read them several times silently or aloud. See what sticks out to you. What new truth is God revealing to you today?

—Day 4—

YOU VS. YOURSELF

As you enter this final personal study, you may be reflecting on the previous days' studies—on your clubs and your "Gentiles" and your attempts to take grace into your own hands. You may be realizing your subconscious tendency to think of some people as "unclean" and yourself as "clean." Or you may be lamenting others' treatment of you as such.

Your grace-a-lot tendencies and habits of forming into exclusive clubs are more a reflection of how you feel about yourself than how you feel about others. It is hard to accept others when you haven't accepted yourself. It is hard to accept grace when you don't think you deserve it. But if it's true that Jesus accepts everyone—that there "is neither Jew nor Gentile, neither slave nor free, nor is there male and female" (Galatians 3:28)—then it's true that Christ accepts the most difficult person for you to accept: *you*.

This internal hesitancy can prevent you from becoming the lighthouse to the world that God desires you to be. This reluctance toward self-acceptance can make grace impossible for you to accept. So, how do you confront yourself and accept what you see? *Choose to see what Christ sees instead*. Believe the truth about who he says you are.

It's true what they say: *you are your own worst enemy*. This is especially true when it comes to having grace for yourself and, therefore, being able to extend grace to others. If you are to be a lighthouse, pointing others to Jesus, you must first believe in the light that is in you, or else you will do what Scripture warns against and hide it (see Matthew 5:14). Self-acceptance isn't just about *you*. It's about how you treat others and how others will see Jesus through you. So believe what he has said about you to be true, accept the free gift of grace he is extending to you, and be transformed in the way you feel about yourself and others.

READ | Jeremiah 31:3, Romans 8:15, 2 Corinthians 5:17, Colossians 2:10, and 1 Peter 2:9

REFLECT

1. These verses are a mix of God speaking to the Israelites and the New Testament writers speaking to the members of the early church.[28] Although they are from different

time periods, they share a common theme. According to these verses, how does God feel about you?

2, Who are you in Christ? List every description that you see in these verses.

3. What parts of you are hard to accept? How might this be holding you back from receiving God's grace and extending that grace to others?

4. Which of these verses do you most need to believe today? Why?

PRAY | As you close your time in prayer, reserve a few minutes to simply sit in Jesus' presence. Listen for his voice. Ask him to help you see who you are in him and how much he loves you.

WRAP IT UP

Use this time to complete any study and reflection questions from previous days this week that you weren't able to finish. Make note of any revelations you've had and reflect on any growth or personal insights you've gained. Finally, discuss with your group what studies you might want to go through next and when you will next meet together.

LEADER'S GUIDE

Thank you for your willingness to lead your group through this study! What you have chosen to do is valuable and will make a great difference in the lives of others. The rewards of being a leader are different from those of participating, and we hope that as you lead you will find your own journey with Christ deepened by this experience.

In the Footsteps of the Savior is a six-session Bible study built around video content and small-group interaction. As the group leader, imagine yourself as the host of a party. Your job is to take care of your guests by managing the details so that when your guests arrive, they can focus on one another and on the interaction around the topic for that session.

Your role as the group leader is not to answer all the questions or reteach the content—the video, book, and study guide will do most of that work. Your job is to guide the experience and cultivate your small group into a connected and engaged community. This will make it a place for members to process, question, and reflect—not necessarily receive more instruction.

There are several elements in this leader's guide that will help you as you structure your study and reflection time, so be sure to follow along and take advantage of each one.

BEFORE YOU BEGIN

Before your first meeting, make sure the group members have a copy of this study guide. Alternately, you can hand out the study guides at your first meeting and give the members some time to look over the material and ask any preliminary questions. Also make sure they are aware that they have access to the streaming videos at any time by following the instructions printed on the inside front cover. During your first meeting, ask the members to provide their name, phone number, and email address so you can keep in touch with them.

Generally, the ideal size for a group is eight to ten people, which will ensure that everyone has enough time to participate in discussions. If you have more people, you might want to break up the main group into smaller subgroups. Encourage those who show up at the first meeting to commit to attending the duration of the study, as this will help the group members get to know one another, create stability for the group, and help you know how to best prepare to lead them through the material.

Each session begins with an opening reflection in the Welcome section. The questions that follow in the Connect section serve as an icebreaker to get the group members thinking about the topic. Some people may want to tell a long story in response to one of these questions, but the goal is to keep the answers brief. Ideally, you want everyone in the group to get a chance to answer, so try to keep the responses to a minute or less. If you have talkative group members, say up front that everyone needs to limit their answer to one minute.

Give the group members a chance to answer, but also tell them to feel free to pass if they wish. With the rest of the study, it's generally not a good idea to have everyone answer every question—a free-flowing discussion is more desirable. But with the opening icebreaker questions, you can go around the circle. Encourage shy people to share, but don't force them.

At your first meeting, let the group members know each session contains a personal study section they can use to continue to engage with the content until the next meeting. While this is optional, it will help them cement the concepts presented during the group study time and help them better understand what it means to follow in the footsteps of the Savior. Let them know that if they choose to do so, they can watch the video for the next session by accessing the streaming code found on the inside front cover of their studies. Invite them to bring any questions and insights to your next meeting, especially if they had a breakthrough moment or didn't understand something.

PREPARATION FOR EACH SESSION

As the leader, there are a few things you should do to prepare for each meeting:

- **Read through the session.** This will help you become more familiar with the content and know how to structure the discussion times.

- **Decide how the videos will be used.** Determine whether you want the members to watch the videos ahead of time (again, via the streaming access code found on the inside front cover) or together as a group.

- **Decide which questions you want to discuss.** Based on the length of your group discussions, you may not be able to get through all the questions. So look over the recommendations for the suggested and additional questions in each session and choose which ones you definitely want to cover.

- **Be familiar with the questions you want to discuss.** When the group meets, you'll be watching the clock, so make sure you are familiar with the questions that you have selected. In this way, you will ensure that you have the material more deeply in your mind than your group members.

- **Pray for your group.** Pray for your group members and ask God to lead them as they study his Word.

In many cases, there will be no one "right" answer to the question. Answers will vary, especially when the group members are being asked to share their personal experiences.

STRUCTURING THE DISCUSSION TIME

You will need to determine how long you want to meet so you can plan your time accordingly. Suggested times for each section have been provided in this study guide, and if you adhere to these times, your group will meet for ninety minutes, as noted below. If you want to meet for two hours, follow the times given in the right-hand column:

Section	90 Minutes	120 Minutes
CONNECT (discuss one or more of the opening questions for the session)	15 minutes	20 minutes
WATCH (watch the teaching material together and take notes)	20 minutes	20 minutes
DISCUSS (discuss the study questions you selected ahead of time)	35 minutes	50 minutes
RESPOND (write down key takeaways)	10 minutes	15 minutes
PRAY (pray together and dismiss)	10 minutes	15 minutes

As the group leader, it is up to you to keep track of the time and keep things on schedule. You might want to set a timer for each segment so both you and the group members know when your time is up. (There are some good phone apps for timers that play a gentle chime or other pleasant sound instead of a disruptive noise.)

Don't be concerned if the group members are quiet or slow to share. People are often quiet when they are pulling together their ideas, and this might be a new experience for them. Just ask a question and let it hang in the air until someone shares. You can then say, "Thank you. What about others? What came to you when you watched that portion of the teaching?"

GROUP DYNAMICS

Leading a group through *In the Footsteps of the Savior* will prove to be highly rewarding both to you and your group members. But you still may encounter challenges along the way! Discussions can get off track. Group members may not be sensitive to the needs and ideas of others. Some might worry they will be expected to talk about matters that make them feel awkward. Others may express comments that result in disagreements. To help ease this strain on you and the group, consider the following ground rules:

- When someone raises a question or comment that is off the main topic, suggest that you deal with it another time, or, if you feel led to go in that direction, let the group know you will be spending some time discussing it.

- If someone asks a question that you don't know how to answer, admit it and move on. At your discretion, feel free to invite group members to comment on questions that call for personal experience.

- If you find one or two people are dominating the discussion time, direct a few questions to others in the group. Outside the main group time, ask the more dominating members to help you draw out the quieter ones. Work to make them a part of the solution instead of part of the problem.

- When a disagreement occurs, encourage the group members to process the matter in love. Encourage those on opposite sides to restate what they heard the other side say about the matter, and then invite each side to evaluate if that perception is accurate. Lead the group in examining other Scriptures related to the topic and look for common ground.

When any of these issues arise, encourage your group members to follow these words from Scripture: "Love one another" (John 13:34), "If it is possible, as far as it depends on you, live at peace with everyone" (Romans 12:18), "Whatever is true . . . noble . . . right . . . if anything is excellent or praiseworthy—think about such things" (Philippians 4:8), and "Be quick to listen, slow to speak and slow to become angry" (James 1:19). This will make your group time more rewarding and beneficial for everyone who attends.

Thank you again for taking the time to lead your group. You are making a difference in your group members' lives and having an impact on their journey as they learn to walk in the footsteps of the Savior in every situation and circumstance in their lives.

ENDNOTES

1. "Capernaum," Wikipedia, https://en.wikipedia.org/wiki/Capernaum; "Capernaum," Tourist Israel, https://www.touristisrael.com/capernaum/7636/#:~:text=In%20Biblical%20times%20Capernaum%20was,Capernaum%20on%20the%20Via%20Maris.

2. Craig S. Keener, *The IVP Bible Background Commentary: New Testament* (Dower's Grove, IL: InterVarsity Press, 1993), 148.

3. Carol A. Newson, Sharon H. Ringe, and Jacqueline E. Lapsley, eds., *Women's Bible Commentary: Twentieth Anniversary Edition* (Louisville: Westminster John Knox Press, 2012), 483.

4. Keener, *The IVP Bible Background Commentary,* 493.

5. James Strong, *Strong's Exhaustive Concordance,* Greek #1544.

6. "Sea of Galilee," Wikipedia, https://en.wikipedia.org/wiki/Sea_of_Galilee; "Josephus," Wikipedia, https://en.wikipedia.org/wiki/Josephus; "Who Was Zebedee in the Bible?", Got Questions, https://www.gotquestions.org/Zebedee-in-the-Bible.html.

7. Keener, *The IVP Bible Background Commentary,* 86.

8. "The Ignatian Examen," Jesuits, https://www.jesuits.org/spirituality/the-ignatian-examen/.

9. Keener, *The IVP Bible Background Commentary,* 87.

10. John Ortberg, *Soul Keeping* (Grand Rapids, MI: Zondervan, 2014), 46.

11. "Mount of Beatitudes," Bible Places, https://www.bibleplaces.com/mtbeatitudes/; "Tabgha," Bible Places, https://www.bibleplaces.com/tabgha/; "Answers," Billy Graham Evangelistic Association, July 30, 2020, https://billygraham.org/answer/does-the-sermon-on-the-mount-cover-the-entire-message-of-jesus-ministry/; "Church of the Beatitudes," Wikipedia, https://en.wikipedia.org/wiki/Church_of_the_Beatitudes.

12. H. R. Jerajani, Bhagyashri Jaju, M. M. Phiske, and Nitin Lade, "Hematohidrosis—A Rare Clinical Phenomenon," National Library of Medicine, July–September 2009, https://www.ncbi.nlm.nih.gov/pmc/articles/PMC2810702/.

13. Keener, *The IVP Bible Background Commentary,* 268.

14. "Southern Steps," Madain Project, https://madainproject.com/southern_steps.

15. "Southern Wall," Wikipedia, https://en.wikipedia.org/wiki/Southern_Wall; "Second Temple," Wikipedia, https://en.wikipedia.org/wiki/Second_Temple; "Southern Steps," Madain Project, https://madainproject.com/southern_steps; "What Was Herod's Temple?", Got Questions, https://www.gotquestions.org/Herod-third-temple.html.

16. John H. Walton, Victor H. Matthews, and Mark W. Chavala, *The IVP Bible Background Commentary: Old Testament* (Dower's Grove, Illinois: InterVarsity Press, 2000), 554.

17. Michael Rogness, "Commentary on Luke 8:26–39," Working Preacher, July 23, 2013, https://www.workingpreacher.org/commentaries/revised-common-lectionary/ordinary-12-3/commentary-on-luke-826-39-3.

18. Keener, *The IVP Bible Background Commentary,* 218.

19. Keener, *The IVP Bible Background Commentary,* 77.

20. Ray Vander Laan, "A New Tomb," That the World May Know, https://www.thattheworldmayknow.com/a-new-tomb.

21. Merrill F. Unger, revised by Gary N. Larson, *The New Unger's Bible Handbook* (Chicago: Moody Press, 1984), 397–398.

22. Oswald Chambers, ed. James Reimann, *My Utmost for His Highest: An Updated Edition in Today's Language* (Grand Rapids: Our Daily Bread Publishing, 1992), April 11.

23. Keener, *The IVP Bible Background Commentary,* 288.

24. "Brief History of Caesarea Maritima," Coral Travel and Tours, https://www.coraltours.org/brief-history-of-caesarea-maritima/; "Caesarea Maritima," Wikipedia, https://en.wikipedia.org/wiki/Caesarea_Maritima#cite_ref-Holum1988_14-0.

25. "Leviticus," The Bible Project, https://bibleproject.com/explore/video/leviticus/.

26. Keener, *The IVP Bible Background Commentary,* 364.

27. Keener, *The IVP Bible Background Commentary,* 364.

28. These verses were taken from a list compiled by Ben Malcomson titled "My Identity in Jesus." Read the full list here: https://storage.googleapis.com/wzukusers/user-29101688/documents/59e7dd73ca5b3XcsdO75/My-Identity-in-Jesus.pdf.

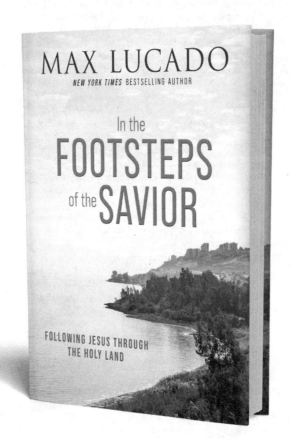